The Art of
Making Jewelry

Thunder Bay Press

An imprint of the Advantage Publishers Group
5880 Oberlin Drive, San Diego, CA 92121-4794
www.thunderbaybooks.com

© 2005 by Quarry Books

All notations of errors or omissions should be addressed to Thunder Bay Press, Editorial Department, at the above address. All other correspondence (author inquiries, permissions) concerning the content of this book should be addressed to Rockport Publishers, Inc., 33 Commercial Street, Gloucester, MA 01930-5089. Telephone: (978) 282-9590; Fax: (978) 283-2742; www.rockpub.com

ISBN-13: 978-1-59223-351-9
ISBN-10: 1-59223-351-1

2 3 4 5 09 08 07 06

Grateful acknowledgment is given to Deborah Krupenia for her work in *The Art of Jewelry Design* (Rockport Publishers, 1997) on pages 198–275; to Tammy Powley for her work in *Making Designer Gemstone and Pearl Jewelry* (Rockport Publishers, 2003) on pages 8–119; and to Jessica Wrobel for her work in *The Paper Jewelry Book* (Rockport Publishers, 1998) on pages 120–195 and 286–304.

Printed in China

The Art of Making Jewelry

Deborah Krupenia · Tammy Powley · Jessica Wrobel

THUNDER BAY
P·R·E·S·S

San Diego, California

Contents

Introduction

Jewelry is the icing on the cake, the flourish of a signature, the ribbon around a wrapped present. Your style may be pared down and austere, or you may lean towards the eclectic and flashy. However you dress, no doubt there is a piece of jewelry that complements your ensemble to a tee. Part how-to guide, part catalog of inspiration, part manual on embellishing yourself—or your loved ones—with peerless works of art, this book is the consummate sourcebook for all jewelry.

Each piece presented here can be viewed as a source of inspiration—a starting point for your own personal expression—or a piece that can be created exactly as described. The charm of making jewelry lies in its process—creating a fresh design, using an exquisite combination of materials, enjoying the fine handwork—all of which engage the senses.

After exploring all these pages have to offer, you may feel inclined to create original designs on your own. Experiment with creative approaches, dabble in exquisite color and texture blends, unearth new embellishments, and crystallize them into a truly one-of-a-kind piece. You are bound only by your creativity!

We invite you to use this book as a guide to the artisan craft of jewelry making, and hope that you enjoy making, wearing, displaying, and giving these beautiful projects. May *The Art of Making Jewelry* inspire and enlighten you, and allow your artistic repertoire to expand.

● selecting supplies

Before you get started making stone jewelry, you will need to collect a number of supplies, including your choice of **beads, findings, and stringing materials.** Below are some basic guidelines to get you started and to help you select the supplies needed to successfully complete the projects in this book. You may also want to refer to this section when you start creating your own jewelry designs. A list of jewelry suppliers can be found on page 280 (Resources).

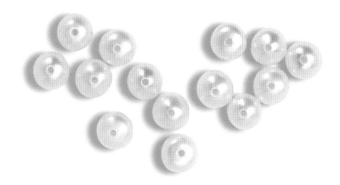

bead basics

Obviously, the most important elements of your jewelry are your beads. They are also the most fun to buy, and there are all kinds of shapes, sizes, and quality of beads on the market today.

SHAPES AND SIZES

Just about any type of stone, from expensive fire opal to economical agate, is available in the form of beads. Round beads are the most common shape of beads, but they come in all kinds of shapes, such as hearts, stars, triangles, and squares. Beads also come in different sizes and are normally measured in millimeters, starting as small as 2 mm. When purchasing large quantities of stone beads, normally they are sold temporarily strung on a 16" (41 cm) string knotted at the end. The number of beads you receive per strand depends on the size of the beads. For round beads, a good rule of thumb is approximately 90 beads for 4 mm, 65 for 6 mm, 50 for 8 mm, and 38 for 10 mm.

QUALITY

When trying to determine the quality of a stone bead, look for irregularities in shape and color. Also, check the holes in the beads. They should be drilled directly down the center of the bead. Look at how the beads line up on the string. Are the beads directly behind each other? If so, then the holes are straight. Normally, your bead vendor will also help you determine the quality of the beads by grading the beads depending on their color and shape. Generally, grade AA is the highest grade, and the lower the quality, the higher up the alphabet the letters go.

ABOUT FINDINGS

In order to connect all your beautiful beads and create jewelry, you need to have an assortment of findings. The majority of the findings used for the projects in this book are made of sterling silver, but findings are available in base metals and precious metals such as gold.

Ear Hooks Ear hooks are used to attach the earring to the wearer's ear and are available in a large variety of designs. Eurowire ear hooks are used for the projects in this book.

Bead Tips Bead tips, also known as clamshells, finish off the ends of strung pieces like bracelets and necklaces.

Jump Rings Jump rings are circles of wire used to connect components such as clasps. They can be made with a little wire, or you can purchase them split open or soldered closed.

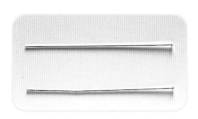

Head Pins Head pins resemble an upside down nail. They are made up of a straight piece of wire with a flat piece, or head, on the end that holds beads in place. Primarily, these are used to make simple earrings.

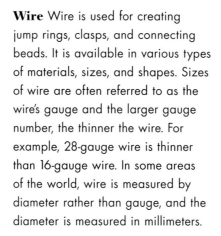

Wire Wire is used for creating jump rings, clasps, and connecting beads. It is available in various types of materials, sizes, and shapes. Sizes of wire are often referred to as the wire's gauge and the larger gauge number, the thinner the wire. For example, 28-gauge wire is thinner than 16-gauge wire. In some areas of the world, wire is measured by diameter rather than gauge, and the diameter is measured in millimeters.

Clasps Clasps come in a huge variety of designs from simple spring ring clasps to fancy toggles and are used to connect the two ends of a piece of jewelry.

Eye Pins Eye pins are similar to head pins but have a small loop, or eye, on the end.

Crimp Beads Crimp beads are small metal beads that are used to finish off beaded necklaces and bracelets.

Chain Chain has an almost infinite number of uses for jewelry making. It is sold by the foot in different designs such as cable link, figaro, or rope.

stringing materials

In order to decide what to string your beads on, you need to first consider what type of beads you are stringing. Unfortunately, there is no single type of stringing material that can do it all. Here is a list of the stringing media used in the jewelry included in this book and the type of beads each works best with.

Silk A well-known classic for bead stringing, silk thread is most often used for pearls. You can purchase silk on large spools or wrapped around cards with an attached needle. It also comes in a variety of colors, such as white, black, gray, and pink, and is available in a range of sizes from a size #1 (.340 mm) to a size #8 (.787 mm).

Nylon When knotting long stone bead necklaces, nylon works very well. Nylon (like silk) can also be purchased on long rolls or on cards with attached needles and comes in different colors and sizes.

Beading Wire Some of the best products in recent development for bead stringing are the various types of coated beading wire. The different brands on the market include Soft Flex, Beadalon, and Accu-Flex, and depending on the manufacturer, there are various sizes and colors available. For the projects in this book that are strung with beading wire, clear Soft Flex, size .014 is used. Beading wire works well with crystals, all types of stone beads, and even the thinner sizes of wire can be used with some pearls.

Memory Wire Though it resembles a slinky, memory wire is actually a coil of steel wire. Normally sold by the ounce, it is available in different sizes (bracelet, necklace, and even ring). Heavy-duty wire cutters or memory wire shears are needed in order to cut loops of this thick wire. I do not recommend that you use your good wire cutter because it will be permanently damaged.

Elastic Stretchy-style jewelry has become very popular, so elastic has entered a new age. It is available in clear and different colors as well as various sizes, which are measured by diameter.

jewelry-making tools

Though there are an endless number of tools available today, some are essential to have in your toolbox. When first starting out, you may use tools you have on hand already, and there is nothing wrong with this. However, once you decide it is time to buy tools exclusively for jewelry making, it is important to purchase a set of quality tools. Many jewelry tools may look similar to tools available in hardware stores, but actually, hand tools used for jewelry are often smaller, lighter, and less bulky than the average tool. Not only will you find quality tools more pleasant to work with, but your finished jewelry will also be more professional in appearance.

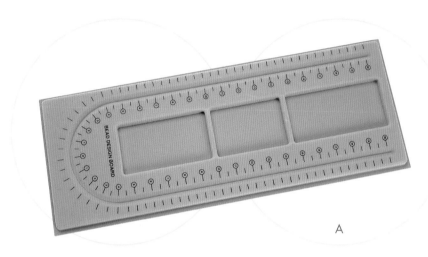

A

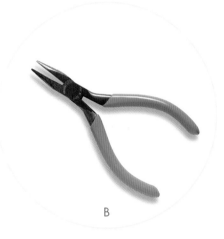

B

Bead Board When designing necklaces and bracelets, a bead board can be indispensable. The "U" shaped groove in the board allows your beads to rest without rolling around, and this allows you to arrange and rearrange your beads until you determine the perfect design. One inch and one-half inch (3 cm and 1 cm) increments are marked around the board to allow you to determine the length of the finished piece. (A).

Flat-Nosed Pliers For bending and gripping wire, flat-nosed pliers are necessary. Make sure you get a pair that is smooth and not textured on the inside of the nose, or this will scratch your wire. (B).

Bent-Nosed Pliers Some jewelry makers prefer to use bent-nosed instead of flat-nosed pliers when working with wire, but it is really a matter of personal preference. Bent-nose pliers are slightly angled at the end of the nose. These pliers are very similar and are used for the same tasks. (C).

Round-Nosed Pliers If you plan to create any sort of curl or loop effect with wire, then round-nosed pliers are a must-have tool. These are made especially for jewelry making, so you will not find them at your local hardware store. The tips of these pliers are cone-shaped, thus providing a smooth area for curling wire. (D).

Crimping Pliers Crimp beads can only be correctly attached to a beaded piece with a pair of crimping pliers.
In fact, crimping pliers are designed only for this task, but it is an important one. These pliers have two notches in the nose that are used to fold and then press the crimp bead. (E).

Nylon-Nosed Pliers If you work with a lot of wire, you may want to eventually purchase a pair of nylon-nosed pliers because they are designed to help straighten kinked and bent wire. While the pliers are metal, the nose of the pliers is made of a hard plastic (nylon) that can be replaced when it gets worn.

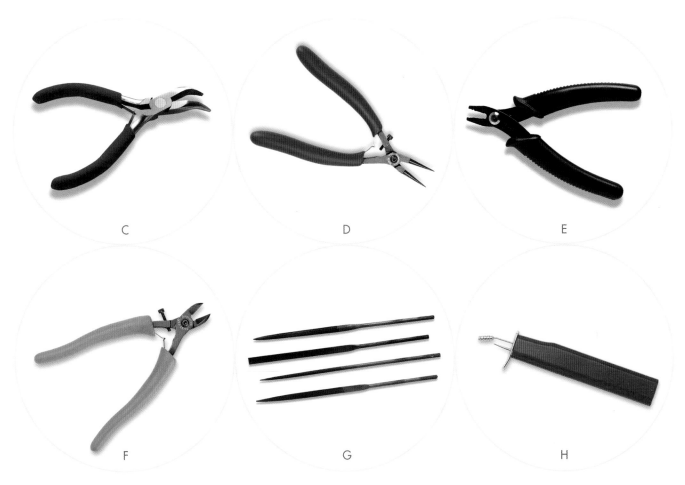

C

D

E

F

G

H

Flush-Cut Wire Cutters Wire cutters are obviously used for cutting wire. However, in order to make sure your wire is cut at a 90-degree angle (so that the end is as flat and smooth as possible), invest in a quality pair of flush-cut wire cutters. This will reduce the amount of filing you will need to do, so in the end, these cutters will not only help you create a quality product but also save you time. (F).

Memory Wire Shears Memory wire is made of steel, so it's very hard and can damage wire cutters. Memory wire shears are created specifically to cut memory wire easily.

Jeweler's Files Even if you use a good pair of wire cutters, you will occasionally need to file the ends of the wire smooth. Jeweler's files are made especially for working with metal. While the technique for using these files is similar to filling your nails, these files are much tougher than an emery board. They normally come in a set of 6 to 12 files in different shapes (flat, round, square, and half-round) and different grits. (G).

Tri-Cord Knotter A specialty tool, the Tri-Cord Knotter is manufactured by the company of the same name and is available from most beading suppliers. This tool has been designed for making the process of knotting between beads quick and easy for a

beginner. Instructions for using this tool are available in the Jewelry Techniques section of this book. (H).

Beading Awl When using the traditional method of knotting between beads, a beading awl is used to help guide and secure the knot between beads.

● jewelry techniques

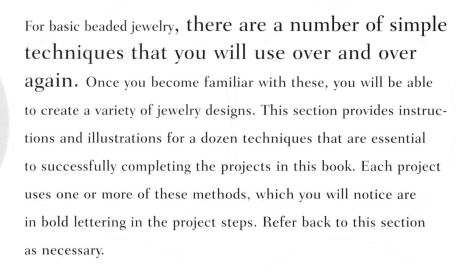

For basic beaded jewelry, **there are a number of simple techniques that you will use over and over again.** Once you become familiar with these, you will be able to create a variety of jewelry designs. This section provides instructions and illustrations for a dozen techniques that are essential to successfully completing the projects in this book. Each project uses one or more of these methods, which you will notice are in bold lettering in the project steps. Refer back to this section as necessary.

bead tips

Bead tips are small metal findings used to start and finish off a beaded piece such as a bracelet or necklace. Some people refer to them as clamshells because they have two cups that are open and look just like a clam. Attached to the cup is a small hook that is used to attach to a clasp or jump ring. You will need to attach bead tips to both the beginning and end of a piece. In addition to bead tips, you will need your choice of cord (such as nylon, silk, or beading wire), flat-nosed pliers, scissors, jeweler's glue, and an awl.

1 To connect a bead tip to the beginning of a piece of beaded jewelry, start by tying at least two overhand knots, one on top of the other, at the end of your cord.

2 Slide the unknotted end of your cord down through the hole in the middle of the bead tip, and pull the cord so that the knots rest inside of one of the shells.

3 Trim off the excess cord, and drop a small amount of glue onto your knots.

4 Use flat-nosed pliers to close the two shells of the bead tip together.

5 Go ahead and string on all of your beads.

6 When you are ready to finish off with a bead tip, add another bead tip to the end of your jewelry piece by slipping the cord through the hole in the bead tip so that the open part of the bead tip (the shell) is facing away from the beads previously strung.

7 Tie a loose overhand knot with your cord, and insert an awl into the knot.

8 Hold the cord with one hand and the awl with your other hand.

9 Use the awl to push the knot down into the bead tip, and pull tightly on your cord with the other hand.

10 Slip the awl out of the knot, and make another knot using this method, making sure that both knots fit inside one of the shells.

11 Trim off the excess cord, and drop a small amount of glue onto your knots.

12 Finish by using flat-nosed pliers to close the two shells of the bead tip together.

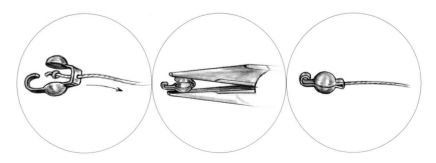

jeweler's tip Clasps are easily attached to bead tips by slipping the clasp's loop onto the bead tip's hook. Then use round-nosed pliers to curl the hook around the loop in order to attach it to the bead tip. Be sure not to flatten the hook, or the clasp will be rigid.

adding crimp beads

A beaded piece of jewelry can be finished on the ends a number of different ways, and using crimp beads to do this is one popular method. Some jewelry makers prefer the look of crimp beads to bead tips, but it is really a matter of personal preference. In order to use this method, a pair of crimping pliers is required. As with bead tips, you need to understand how to start and finish with crimp beads because there are a few minor differences. In addition to crimping pliers, you will also need crimp beads (I highly recommend using tube-shaped crimp beads versus round crimp beads because they are much easier to work with), round-nosed pliers, wire cutters, and beading wire.

1 Slide one crimp bead onto the end of a piece of beading wire, and loop the wire back through the crimp bead.

2 Position the crimp bead inside the second notch in the crimping pliers (the one closest to you when you are holding the pliers in your hand), and close the pliers around the bead. You should see the crimp bead now has a groove down the middle so that it curls.

3 Now, position the same crimp bead in the first notch in the pliers, and close the pliers around it so that you are flattening the curl.

4 Using wire cutters, trim off all but about ¼" (5 mm) of excess beading wire.

5 Add your beads making sure to slide the first bead over both pieces of wire on the end.

6 Once you have all of your beads on, you are ready to finish the other end. Slide a

second crimp bead onto the end of your wire and push it up against the last bead strung.

7 Loop the wire back through the crimp bead as well as the last bead of the piece.

8 Insert the nose of your round-nosed pliers into the loop.

9 While holding your round-nosed pliers with one hand, gently pull the beading wire with your other hand so that you push the crimp bead up against the other beads. This will ensure that you do not have any extra slack in your beaded piece and that you also keep the end loop of your beading wire in tact.

10 Repeat steps 2 and 3 above to close the crimp bead.

11 Finish by using wire cutters to carefully trim off excess beading wire.

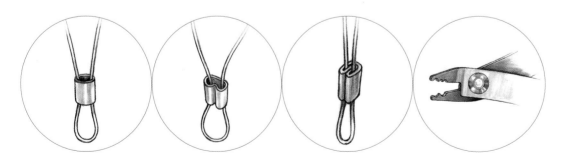

jeweler's tip

Tube-shaped crimp beads are available in sterling, gold-filled, and gold, while round-shaped crimp beads normally come in base metals. However, the most important reason for using tube-shaped crimp beads is that they are easier to work with. Therefore, the majority of beginners have better results with them.

traditional knotting

Knotting between beads is a technique used by many jewelry makers when stringing high-end beads such as pearls. The knots between the beads allow for a nice draping effect when finished, and they also have a practical purpose. If a knotted necklace were to break, the beads would not roll off the strand. Also, they create a little space between the beads so that they do not rub against each other. This is especially important for pearls or other soft beads. In order to knot between your beads, you need a beading awl (a corsage pin also works well), silk or nylon cord with an attached, twisted wire needle, and your choice of beads.

1 Start by finishing one end of your cord in the technique you prefer. I normally use the Bead Tip Technique (page 15) for this.

2 Once your necklace is started, string on your first bead and push it down to the end of your necklace.

3 Now, tie a loose overhand knot.

4 Insert your beading awl through the loose knot.

5 Next, use one hand to push the awl and knot down toward the bead and hold onto the cord with your other hand until the awl and knot are flush up against the bead.

6 Keeping the knot up against the bead, carefully slip the end of your awl out of the knot and immediately use your fingers to push the knot against the bead.

7 Repeat this method for each bead that you wish to knot between.

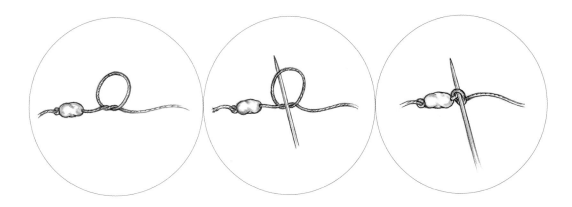

jeweler's tip If you are a beginner or plan to knot only occasionally, then I recommend using the commercially available cord that includes an attached, twisted wire needle (see Resources, page 280). However, if you plan to do a lot of knotting, then you may want to invest in large spools of cord and separate needles because this will be more economical. As with all techniques, knotting takes a good deal of practice in order to get consistent results.

tri-cord knotter

For those who are new to knotting, this tool can save a lot of time and frustration. It is made specifically for knotting between beads, and while it does take some practice to learn to use, it can save the beginner a lot of time. Many jewelry supply vendors sell this tool and an instructional video. To knot with the Tri-Cord Knotter, you will also need your choice of beads and some nylon or silk cord with an attached twisted wire needle.

1 Start by finishing one end of your cord in the technique you prefer. I normally use the bead tip technique (see page 15) for this. Once your necklace is started, string on your first bead and push it down to the end of your necklace. Now, tie a loose overhand knot.

2 Hold the knotter tool in one hand so that your thumb is resting up against the metal lip that extends out at the top of the knotter. Insert the awl tip of your tool into the your overhand knot.

3 Still grasping the wooden handle of the knotter, push the knot and awl tip up against your bead while you hold onto the cord with your other hand.

4 Take the cord you are holding and position it in the V-groove of the knotter.

5 Continue to keep the tension on the cord while you use the thumb of your other hand to push up on the metal lip of the knotter. This will force your knot to come off of your awl tip and rest tightly up against your bead.

6 Repeat this method for each bead that you wish to knot between.

jeweler's tip

Just because you have a tool to make knotting easier and faster does not mean you will have perfect results the first time. However, with practice and a little patience you will have professional looking knots very soon.

square knots

Most often used for finishing off beads strung on elastic cord, the traditional square knot is one of the strongest and easiest techniques. You are probably already familiar with making this type of knot.

1 Position the ends of your cord in the shape of an X so that the right end is over the left end of the cord.

2 Bring the right cord over and under the other end of your cord, and pull both ends tightly so that you have the first part of the knot completed.

3 Repeat step 1, but instead position the left end is over the right end of the cord.

4 Bring the left cord over and under the other end of your cord, and pull both ends tightly to complete the knot.

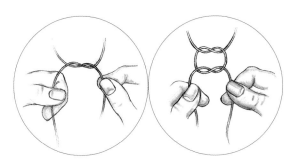

jeweler's tip

Depending on the size of your cord, you may want to tie more than one square knot, one on top of the other, to make your jewelry piece secure. Also, do not forget that you can hide your knots inside beads; just make sure to use a bead with a large enough hole.

using jeweler's files

When using wire to create jewelry components, such as dangles or clasps, you may notice sometimes that the ends of your wire can cut or poke the wearer of the jewelry. Therefore, it is very helpful to use a jeweler's file to smooth the ends. When using a jeweler's file, the method is very similar to that of filing nails.

1 After cutting a piece of wire, run the file in one direction against the end that was cut.

2 After making a piece of jewelry that uses wire, use your fingers to double-check the wire areas (such as wrap loops for example) to ensure that the wire is smooth. If you feel a rough spot, run the file in one direction against this area again.

jeweler's tip

Remember to file in one direction, never back and forth. Though some of the smaller wire (24–28-guage or .50 mm to .33 mm) may not require filing, always check your wire ends to make sure. You want your jewelry to be both attractive and comfortable to wear.

making jump rings

Jump rings are used for connecting numerous jewelry components. A simple jump ring can even be combined with a hook and be used as a clasp. While these can also be purchased fairly inexpensively, sometimes it can be very handy to be able to create your own jump rings. The size of the jump rings you make depends on the diameter of the dowel, and the number of jump rings you make will depend on the amount of wire used. To make jump rings, you will need a wooden dowel (a pencil or pen works well also), flush-cut wire cutters, a jeweler's file, and at least 6" (15 cm) of wire.

1 Begin by using your fingers to wrap your wire around your dowel so that the wire is flush against it.

2 Then slide the wire off the dowel so that you have a coil of wire.

3 Take a pair of flush-cut wire cutters and cut each coil one time to create a single ring.

4 Finally, take a jeweler's file and smooth the ends of the wire just cut so that both ends of the jump ring are flat and can fit flush together.

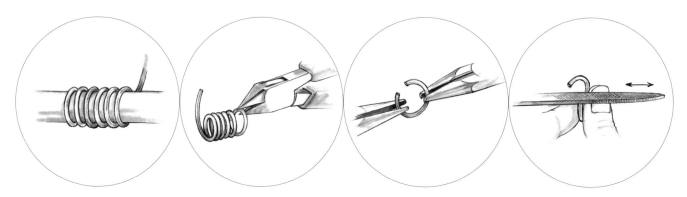

jeweler's tip

If you decided to purchase jump rings rather than make them yourself, you can buy them closed (soldered) or open (unsoldered). So, consider the project you plan to use them for before purchasing.

wrap loop

The wrap loop technique is extremely useful for a large number of jewelry projects. You can use it to make earrings, add dangles to necklaces, create bead and wire chain, or finish off a clasp for a bracelet. For this technique, you will need a pair of round-nosed pliers, wire cutters, flat-nosed pliers, a jeweler's file, and your choice of wire to create wrap loops.

1 Start by using the flat-nosed pliers to bend the wire to a 90-degree angle so that you create an upside down L-shape.

2 Position the nose of your round-nosed pliers in the bend, which you created in the previous step.

3 Use your fingers to wrap the wire around the nose of your pliers to form a loop.

4 While you are keeping the round-nosed pliers inside the loop, hold the loop against the nose of the pliers with one finger. So, you should have your round-nosed pliers in one hand with one finger pressing the loop against the nose. (If you are right handed, then you will probably want to use your left hand to hold the pliers and your pointer finger to hold the loop against the nose.)

5 Using your other hand (if right handed, the right hand), start to wrap the loose wire around the straight piece of wire that is directly under your loop. If the wire is soft,

you can probably do this with your fingers. Otherwise, use a flat-nosed (or bent-nosed if you prefer) pair of pliers to hold the loose wire and wrap.

6 Continue to wrap as many times as you want, and if necessary, trim off excess wire and file smooth with a jeweler's file.

7 Use your flat-nosed pliers to press the wire-wrapped end flat to make sure it does not scratch or poke the wearer of your jewelry.

8 If necessary, use your round-nosed pliers to straighten the loop.

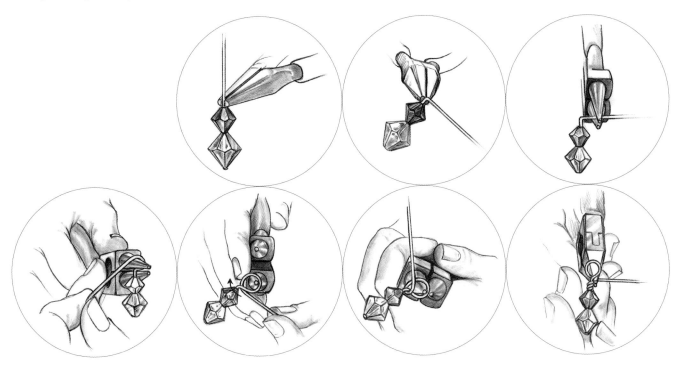

● **jeweler's tip**

Be patient, and be prepared to practice. There is no way you will do this perfectly the first time. The more you do it, the better you will become. Be careful not to wrap too closely to a bead if you are including one on the wire as it could crack the bead. Though some jewelry makers like to get their wrap as close as possible to the bead, I do not mind a little room, but this is personal preference. Also, when making long loop-wrapped chains, instead of cutting lots of small pieces of wire for each loop, try using longer pieces (about 12" [30 cm] or so in length) and then cutting the wire after each loop is made. This will keep wire waste down.

simple loop

This technique is a simplified version of the wrap loop technique and is useful for making earrings, dangles, pendants, and various other jewelry components. While wrapping is more secure, if done properly, this simple loop technique can also be surprisingly strong. For this procedure, you will need a pair of round-nosed pliers, wire cutters, and a head pin. Though a head pin is being used for illustration purposes, you can also use this technique with wire.

1 First, use your round-nosed pliers to bend the head pin at a 90-degree angle.

2 Make sure that the part of the head pin that is bent is about ½" (1 cm) long, and if necessary, trim any excess with wire cutters.

3 Position the bent part of the head pin so that it is facing away from you.

4 Then, using round-nosed pliers, grasp the end of the bent head pin and make

sure that the middle part of the plier's nose is holding the pin.

5 After positioning your pliers correctly, slowly curl the wire toward you.

6 Since the first curl will probably not complete the circle yet, release and reposition your pliers on the circle you have started.

7 Continue to curl it toward you until you have made a circle.

> **jeweler's tip** When trying this the first time, you may not get a perfect circle. It will take a little practice. However, once you have it, you will get better and better at it until you have nice round loops on the end of your wire or head pin.

figure eight eye

By using a little wire, you can fashion this simple figure eight design. The two loops on this piece combine to work as the second part of a clasp, which is made to team up with any number of hook-style clasps. To make a figure eight eye, you will need approximately 1½" (4 cm) of wire, a jeweler's file, and round-nosed pliers.

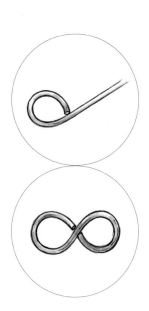

1 Start by using a jeweler's file to smooth both ends of your wire.

2 Now use your round-nosed pliers to make a large loop on one end of the wire so that you have used up half of the piece of wire.

3 Do the same on the other end of the wire, but this time the loop should be facing in the other direction so that you make a figure eight with the wire.

> **jeweler's tip** These pieces can be added to a beaded jewelry piece whether it is finished with a bead tip or a crimp bead. For bead tips, just hook the bead tip onto one of the loops of the figure eight eye and close the hook around it. If you use a crimp bead, you can use pliers to slightly open one end of your figure eight eye, slip the beading wire loop onto it, and then close it back up.

"s" hook adapter

The "S" design is a very versatile wire shape that can be used for all kinds of components. It works as a clasp and can also be used as an adapter so that a beaded jewelry piece can have more than one function (as illustrated in the Adaptable Amber Eye Chain project, page 38). All you need is about 2" (5 cm) of wire, a jeweler's file, and round-nosed pliers.

1 Start by using a jeweler's file to smooth the ends of your wire.

2 Take your round-nosed pliers, place the nose of the pliers a little higher than half way down the wire, and curl one end of the wire around the nose to create a hook shape.

3 Repeat this on the other end of the wire so that the hook is facing in the opposite direction.

4 Again use round-nosed pliers to make the smallest possible curls on both ends of your wire hooks.

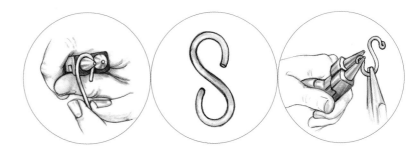

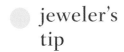 **jeweler's tip**

For a different look to your adapter, try using square instead of round wire. This will add to your design, and the basic method used to create the adapter is the same.

hook with wrap

You can make your own clasp by teaming up this hook with the figure eight eye. This method combines two techniques: The "S" hook adapter and the wrap loop. Therefore, once you learn these first two methods, you will find this hook very easy to make. You will need about 3" (8 cm) of wire, a jeweler's file, wire cutters, flat-nosed pliers, and round-nosed pliers.

1 Use a jeweler's file to smooth the ends of the wire.

2 As described in steps 2 and 4 of the "S" hook adapter (above), use round-nosed pliers to create a hook and then a curl on one end of your wire.

3 Now, using the wrap loop technique (page 20), create a large wrap loop on the opposite end of the hook you just made.

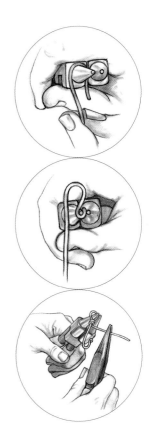

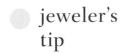 **jeweler's tip**

You may need to think ahead in a design sometimes. For example, if you plan to connect a hook with wrap to a piece of chain (or other item that cannot be opened), remember not to close your loop on the hook until after you connect it to the chain. So, you would start your wrap, slip on the chain, and then finish your wrap. However, if you use this on the end of a piece of jewelry that uses a bead tip, you will just connect the hook of the bead tip around the loop of your hook after it has been wrapped.

Working with Gemstones and Pearls

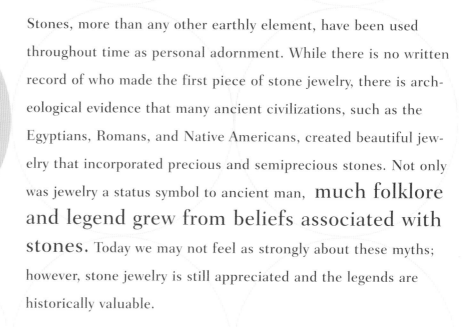

Stones, more than any other earthly element, have been used throughout time as personal adornment. While there is no written record of who made the first piece of stone jewelry, there is archeological evidence that many ancient civilizations, such as the Egyptians, Romans, and Native Americans, created beautiful jewelry that incorporated precious and semiprecious stones. Not only was jewelry a status symbol to ancient man, **much folklore and legend grew from beliefs associated with stones.** Today we may not feel as strongly about these myths; however, stone jewelry is still appreciated and the legends are historically valuable.

This book connects stone folklore from the past with classic as well as trendy jewelry designs for the modern jewelry lover. I designed each piece of jewelry around four stone-related powers: **love, strength, wisdom, and peace.** Therefore, you will find the projects in this section organized by the stones they incorporate. The Jewelry Techniques section on page 14 offers step-by-step instructions for the methods used throughout. Refer to this section for specific techniques, which you will find in bold print in each project. While the instructions and projects are easy enough for a beginner to follow, any level of jewelry maker will find the projects in this book fun to make. I hope you enjoy the power of creativity you can gain from making your own stone bead jewelry.

Following is a list of stones and the powers associated with each one. You will find many of them included in the project section of this book along with more historical and mythical information.

Agate
Powers include strength, courage, longevity, love, healing, and protection.

Amazonite Provides the powers of truth, honor, love, confidence, and sincerity. (Not shown.)

Amber
Actually fossilized tree sap, not a stone; powers include luck, healing, strength, protection, and love.

Amethyst
Makes the wearer gentle and amiable

Aventurine Worn to strengthen the eyes, stimulate creativity, and enhance intelligence. (Not shown.)

Aquamarine
Assists in thoughtfulness, visualization, peace, and motivation.

Beryl
Amplifies persistence, charity, thoughtfulness, wisdom, and clarity.

Carnelian Promotes peace and harmony, and dispels depression. (Not shown.)

Chrysocolla
Evokes affirmation, love, and understanding.

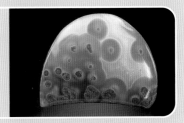

Chrysoprase
Powers include strength, enthusiasm, and clear communication.

Citrine
Powers include nightmare prevention, protection, and psychic ability.

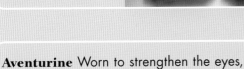

Crystal Quartz Powers include healing, wisdom, and harmony. (Not shown.)

Fluorite
Works with the conscious mind to calm, increase wisdom, and balance.

Lapis
Assists with strength, purity of heart, and courage.

Garnet
Powers include healing, love, friendship, protection, and strength.

Limestone Powers include of protection, longevity, culture, and purity. (Not shown.)

Hematite Makes the wearer alert; powers include concentration, self-control, courage, and self-confidence. (Not shown.)

Malachite
Powers include protection, love, peace, wisdom, and leadership.

Howlite Encourages creativity, self-expression, and unity. (Not shown.)

Moonstone
Enhances joy, fortune, and peacefulness.

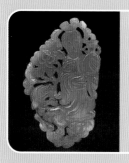

Jade
A love-attracting stone used since ancient times; powers include fertility, balance, and wisdom.

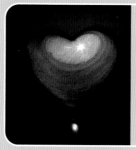

Obsidian
Powers include protection, peace, success, and inner contemplation.

Jasper Powers include healing, protection, health, relaxation, solace, and beauty. (Not shown.)

Onyx Protects, strengthens, and energizes. (Not shown.)

Pearls
Powers include love, money, protection, luck, purity, and honesty.

Peridot
Powers include protection, health, wealth, and sleep.

Rhodonite
Worn to calm, cast off doubt, provide peace, and remove confusion.

Rose Quartz Attracts love, promotes peace, happiness, and fidelity. (Not shown.)

Sodalite Powers include healing, peace, meditation, and wisdom. (Not shown.)

Sugilite Encourages strength, safety, healing, and wisdom. (Not shown.)

Tiger's-Eye
Powers include courage, energy, and luck.

Topaz
Protects and heals the wearer, brings peace, money, and love.

Turquoise
Powers include protection, courage, peace, healing, and luck.

Unakite
Promotes emotional balance, love, and healing.

Zoizite Encourages thought, dreams, peace, and meditation. (Not shown.)

love

Whether you are thinking about your knight in shining armor or the closeness you feel for a friend or family member, love is one of the most powerful emotions we experience. We all want love, and we all need love. Perhaps this is why so many semi-precious stones are linked to this strong emotion. Some of the stones associated with love include rose quartz, amazonite, jade, garnet, amber, and chryso-colla. While there is no guaran-tee that wearing one of these stones will bring you love, the fact that you can incorporate these love stones into your own jewelry to give to a friend or loved one adds special meaning to your finished piece of jewelry.

The idea of sitting down and cre-ating a piece of jewelry for one particular person is, in itself, an act of love. Selecting just the right stones, arranging all the components, and then assembling the piece bead by bead adds an uncommon element to each jew-elry item you make. As you work with your hands to create jewelry, you can think about how much enjoyment the wearer will receive from your handcrafted symbol of affection.

Each project in this chapter has been designed around the theme of love and friendship. Not only are the stones used in the jewelry related to love, but small details like the use of heart-shaped beads and flower clasps add a distinc-tive touch that will show how much care was put into each piece of jewelry you create.

circle of love necklace

An ancient love-attracting stone, jade has long been an important part of Asian culture. Jade is also believed to prolong life, aid in fertility, and provide the wearer with a sense of balance and wisdom. Cut in the shape of a circle, symbolizing eternal love, this ornately carved piece of jade is combined with amazonite, amethyst, and crystal beads.

Amazonite is also associated with love as well as truth and honor. Its name comes from the Amazon River because it was once believed to originate there. However, this stone is found around the world including the United States, Brazil, Australia, and Africa. Amethyst beads, believed to make the wearer gentle, alternate between the amazonite beads in this piece which measures about 21" (53 cm) long.

materials

- one 30-mm doughnut jade circle with 4 drilled holes
- two 2" (5 cm) 20-gauge (.80-mm) head pins
- four 6-mm emerald-colored square crystal beads
- six 4-mm amethyst-colored bi-cone crystal beads
- nine 6-mm amazonite beads
- twenty-four 8-mm amazonite beads
- thirty-one 4-mm amethyst beads
- 2 bead tips
- 2' (0.6 m) of beading wire
- **hook with wrap**
- **figure eight eye**
- round-nosed pliers
- flat-nosed pliers
- wire cutters
- nylon-nosed pliers

step by step

1 Begin by creating the pendant component of this necklace. Take your jade bead and locate the holes that have been drilled through the circle. I used one with four holes: one at the top of the circle, two in the center of the circle across from each other, and one at the bottom of the circle.

2 Take a head pin and insert it through two of these holes, starting with the hole in the center area of the circle and going up through the top hole on the outer edge of the circle. The "head" of the pin should be flush against the center hole.

3 Slip one 6-mm amazonite bead and one 4-mm amethyst bead onto your head pin that is now coming out of the top of your stone circle.

4 Using your round- and flat-nosed pliers, create a **wrap loop** with the rest of the head pin.

5 Take a second head pin and insert it down through the other two holes, again starting with the hole in the center so that the head is flush up against this hole.

6 Slip one 4-mm amethyst bead onto the pin.

7 Now use your round-nosed pliers to make a small curl on the end of your head pin.

8 Use either your fingers (the wire of the head pin is soft) or nylon-nosed pliers to continue curling the pin until it rests up against the amethyst bead.

9 Set your pendant aside to be used later.

10 Attach a **bead tip** onto one end of your beading wire.

11 Now string on the following beads, which will be referred to from now on as pattern A: Alternate one 4-mm amethyst bead and one 8-mm amazonite bead four times and then end with one 4-mm amethyst bead.

12 Next, string on the following beads which will be referred to from now on as pattern B: One 6-mm amazonite bead, one 4-mm amethyst-colored crystal bead, one 6-mm emerald-colored crystal bead, one 4-mm amethyst-colored crystal bead, and one 6-mm amazonite bead.

13 Repeat pattern A, then pattern B, and than pattern A again.

14 You are now ready to add your pendant. Slip the loop of the pendant onto the beading wire.

15 Repeat steps 11 through 13 for the other side of your necklace.

16 Finish off the beading wire with a bead tip.

17 Finally, attach a **hook with wrap** to one bead tip and **figure eight eye** to the other bead tip.

jeweler's tip

Besides jade, stone circles are available in a large variety of semiprecious stones such as jasper, onyx, rose quartz, and agate. Often, suppliers also refer to these as donuts. Sizes normally range from 20 mm up to 40 mm or even larger. The smaller circles are excellent for creating earrings and bracelets. When selecting a stone circle or donut, be careful to examine the edges of the circle to ensure there are no chips. If not packaged correctly, the edges are where these pieces can most often become damaged.

❱❱ variation

Amethyst beads are teamed up with leopardskin jasper to create another unusual color combination, but instead of the bright green of amazonite, this leopardskin jasper stone has earthy hues of gray, brown, black, and tan mixed together. This stone jasper circle does not have any additional holes drilled through it. Therefore, in order to create the pendant, about 5" (13 cm) of 22-gauge (.65 mm) round sterling silver wire was bent in half to go through and then around the circle. The two ends of the wire were then wrapped around each other when they met at the top of the circle. Finally, the **wrap loop** technique was used to finish the top of the pendant.

gem folklore

Jasper is an opaque form of chalcedony, which is mined in many countries but primarily comes from areas of Brazil and Uruguay. Some of the powers affiliated with jasper include healing, protection, and relaxation. This stone has a rich history of use in symbolic rituals. Native Americans used jasper in rain ceremonies. As a talisman, ancient people wore jasper to suppress threatening desires. Mothers-to-be held a piece of jasper to protect and heal them during childbirth. Perhaps the reason jasper was used for so many purposes is because not only does it come in a mixture of earth tones, but it also comes in an array of colors, such as bright shades of green and red.

it's a bracelet—
it's a necklace

Both a necklace and a bracelet, this 21" (53 cm) beaded jewelry piece is very versatile. You can **wear it as a necklace, or you can wrap it around your wrist three times, thus creating a multistrand bracelet.** While garnets are the primary stone beads in this piece, other assorted beads (stone, crystal, glass, metal, ceramic, you name it) are used as accents throughout.

The more eclectic it is, the better. Garnets work well with almost any other bead, so they serve to visually unify the various beads in this design. They also have a strong connection to the power of love because garnets were **once commonly exchanged between parting friends to symbolize their affection and ensure that they would meet again.**

materials

- one 16" (41 cm) strand of 4-mm garnet beads
- assortment of accent beads
- garnet-colored nylon beading cord, size 4, with attached needle

- 2 sterling silver bead tips
- 1 sterling silver toggle clasp
- jeweler's cement
- scissors
- bead board

- flat-nosed pliers
- round-nosed pliers
- beading awl

step by step

1 First lay your garnet beads on your bead board and spread them out, starting from the 10 ½" (27 cm) mark on one side and ending at the 10 ½" (27 cm) mark on the other side of the board. You will not have enough garnet beads to cover the area between the 10 ½" (27 cm) marks on your board, so do not concern yourself with spreading out the garnet beads evenly. The reason for this will become clear in the next step.

2 Now comes the fun part—designing. Start adding your accent beads to the empty areas in between your garnet beads. You will probably need to take out a number of the garnet beads to make room for lots of accent beads. Do not worry about symmetry. In fact, try to avoid anything symmetrical. Also, be generous with the accent beads.

3 Take your nylon cord and attach a **bead tip** to one end.

4 String on your beads in the order you have placed them on the bead board. As you string them on, occasionally measure the portion you have strung. The length may not be the same as it was on the board due to the fact that your beads are all different sizes and shapes. If you find you want it longer, add some of the garnet beads you removed previously or add other accent beads.

5 When you have finished stringing, measure your piece to ensure it is approximately 21" (53 cm) long, and finish the other end with your second **bead tip**.

6 Finally, add one part of the toggle clasp to one end of your beaded piece by using round-nosed pliers to close the hook of the bead tip around the loop of your toggle section. If necessary, use your flat-nosed pliers to finish closing the loop, being careful not to flatten the loop.

7 Repeat the above step for the other end of your beaded piece and the second part of your toggle clasp to complete the jewelry piece.

jeweler's tip

To create your own variation of this design, it is a good idea to first decide on the primary bead to be used. While garnets and pearls are excellent choices, amethyst, black onyx, or mother-of-pearl beads would also work well. For accent beads, consider leftover beads from past jewelry projects. This is a great way to use up odds and ends, and it also allows you to reconfigure this basic design in a number of different ways so no two are ever alike. Different stringing materials can also be used, such as beading wire or silk; just make sure it is strong and allows for a lot of movement since you want the wearer to be able to wrap the piece around her wrist if desired.

gem folklore

Garnet is a very common stone and can be found in many areas of the world including the United States, India, Brazil, and Australia. Though it is not the most valuable of semiprecious stones, it is extremely popular and often used in fine jewelry. It also has a strong historical and mythological background. During the nineteenth century, garnets became very fashionable. Legends claim that garnets are healing stones and can cure skin problems and help regulate blood flow. Other powers associated with this stone include protection and strength.

⌃ variation

Janice Parsons of beadshop.com used beautiful gold-colored pearls to turn an eclectic, funky design into a classy, sophisticated piece of jewelry. Along with traditional round pearls, she used square-shaped gold pearl beads, crystal beads, and gold-filled findings and accent beads, which she strung on beading wire and finished off with crimp beads. While her choice of beads dresses this piece up, Janice kept to the basic design by arranging her beads to create an asymmetrical mixture. It is also 21" (53 cm), like the main project. Whether worn on the wrist or as a necklace, this is another one-of-a-kind piece.

adaptable amber
eye-glass chain

Both pearls and amber are classified as organic gemstones because they naturally develop through a biological process rather than forming from minerals, as stones do. Amber is actually preserved tree resin that is tens of millions of years old. The Romans called it *succinum* which is Latin for "juice." **Powers associated with amber include love and healing, while pearls are also thought to bring love and have powers of purity and peace.**

Pearls are created in nature when a piece of sand or other foreign body makes its way into an oyster. To protect itself, the oyster covers the foreign matter in layers of what eventually becomes a pearl. The combination of these two organic gemstones is used in this eye-glass chain and accented with olive-colored crystal beads and sterling daisy spacers. Additionally, a small amount of wire formed in an "S" shape allows this chain to be adapted into a necklace.

materials

- thirty 7" x 9" (18 cm x 23 cm) amber leaf-shaped beads
- thirty-one 4-mm pearl beads
- sixty-two 4-mm sterling silver daisy spacers
- thirty-two 4-mm olive-colored crystal beads

- 2 crimp beads
- 2 woven cord eyeglass holders with 6-mm beads
- 30" (76 cm) of beading wire
- 2" (5 cm) of 20-gauge (.08 mm) wire
- crimping pliers

- wire cutters
- round-nosed pliers
- flat-nosed pliers
- jeweler's file

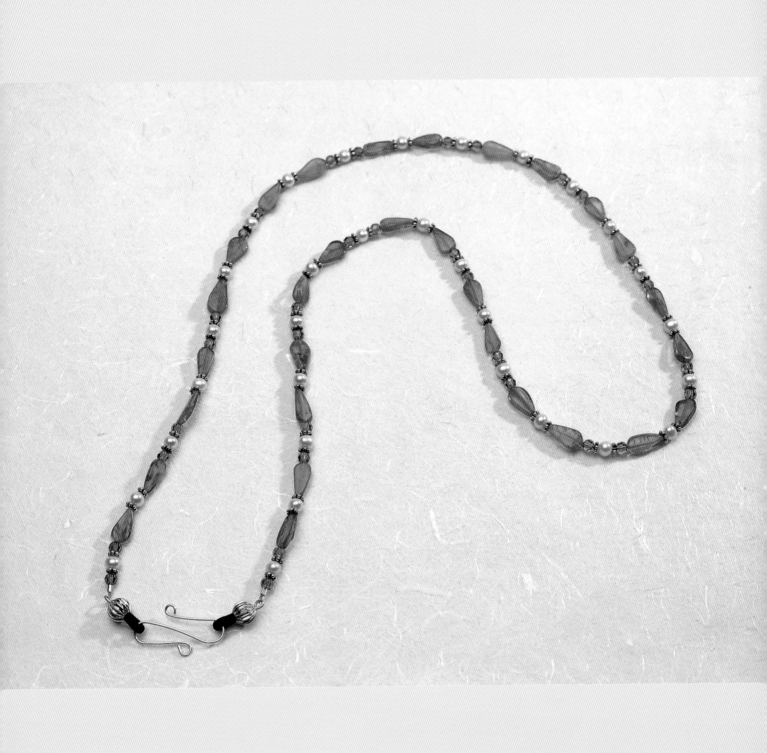

step by step

1 First, attach a **crimp bead** to one end of your beading wire.

2 Now, use round-nosed pliers to open the loop on one of the eyeglass holders.

3 Slip the beading wire loop (created when you attached the crimp) onto the loop of the eyeglass holder, and then use round-nosed pliers to close the holder's loop so that it is secured to the beading wire loop. If necessary, use flat-nosed pliers to secure the loop closed.

4 You are now ready to start stringing on your beads, which are a combination of two bead patterns. Pattern A refers to the following configuration of beads: one olive crystal bead, one daisy spacer, one pearl, one daisy spacer, and one olive crystal bead. Pattern B refers to this configuration of beads: one amber leaf bead, one daisy spacer, one pearl, one daisy spacer, and one amber leaf bead.

5 Next start with pattern A and alternate with pattern B until you have strung on 16 sections of pattern A and 15 sections of pattern B. Make sure that the pointed end of the amber leaf beads are positioned so that they both point inward toward the pearl and spacer beads.

6 Once you have all your beads on, ending with pattern B, you are ready to secure the opposite end with another crimp bead.

7 Repeat steps 2 and 3 to attach the second eyeglass holder onto your bead chain.

8 Finally, make your wire **"S" hook adapter** using round-nosed pliers.

9 To wear the piece as a necklace, secure the woven cord on the eyeglass holders onto either side of the "S" adapter, thus creating a clasp for your necklace. To wear it as an eyeglass chain, slip the woven cord sections onto the frame of your glasses.

jeweler's tip

Most beading supply vendors sell the eyeglass holders needed for this project. While there are a number of different styles available, the bead and woven cord design seems to hold up the best. Rubber eyeglass holders, on the other hand, do not last very long.

Many are secured with a metal coil that can eventually become loose. Remember that if worn regularly, the holders will be stretched each time a person takes the chain on and off a pair of glasses. So, it is important to get the most secure style of eyeglass holders available.

gem folklore

Along with love and healing, amber is thought to bring powers of protection, strength, and luck. It symbolizes life because small animals, such as insects, were sometimes caught in the sap before it hardened. Colors of this organic gemstone range from light honey to darker oranges and browns. Though amber can be found in parts of Poland and Sicily, the Baltic Sea is best known for having chunks of amber floating throughout. Therefore, one test for distinguishing real amber from simulated amber (which is often made from plastic) is to see if it floats in salt water.

variation Classic pearls are used in this variation. Instead of 4-mm round pearls, smaller button pearls are used and accented with sterling silver daisy spacer beads. Faceted 5 mm x 7 mm garnet cube-shaped beads are the predominant beads used in this eyeglass chain variation. As with the original design, this variation is approximately 24" (61 cm) in length, which allows for glasses to rest a few inches (5 cm to 8 cm) below the collarbone. If the chain was any longer, then the glasses could be damaged or become tangled in the chain.

hearts and roses necklace

The color of pink immediately brings to mind femininity and love. This could be one reason why **rose quartz, a pale, milky-pink stone, is believed to attract love and promote peace, happiness, and fidelity in established relationships.** It can be found in Brazil, the United States, and Madagascar. In addition to the use of rose quartz in bringing across the theme of love in this necklace, hematite heart-shaped beads and lampwork beads dotted with little roses add to the romantic look.

The term "lampwork" refers to glass beads which have been created by a lampwork artist who uses a torch to heat rods of glass. Hematite also has a mythological connection to love because it enhances passionate desires. Of course, **roses have long been given to those we love as a sign of our affection.** Finally, a heart and arrow toggle clasp finishes off this beautiful necklace, which has been hand-knotted in sections to ensure the beads are secure and the piece has a graceful drape when worn.

materials

- twenty-one 8-mm rose quartz beads
- fourteen 6-mm rose quartz beads
- fourteen 6-mm hematite heart beads
- fourteen 4-mm clear aurora bore-alis crystal beads
- 7 lampwork beads with rose design

- 1 heart and arrow toggle clasp
- one 5-mm jump ring
- 2 bead tips
- jeweler's cement
- one #4 pale pink carded beading thread (nylon or silk) with attached needle

- scissors
- Tri-Cord Knotter or awl
- round-nosed pliers
- flat-nosed pliers

step by step

1 To begin the necklace, add a **bead tip** to the end of your cord.

2 Then string on three 8-mm rose quartz beads and one 4-mm crystal bead, and use either **traditional knotting** or **Tri-Cord Knotter** to tie a knot.

3 Add a hematite heart bead, making sure that the point of the heart is facing away from the crystal bead.

4 Tie another knot, and then slip on one 6-mm rose quartz bead, one lampwork rose bead, and another 6-mm rose quartz bead.

5 Now tie a knot, string on a heart bead, tie another knot, and string on one 4-mm crystal bead.

6 Repeat steps 2 through 5 two more times.

7 Next repeat steps 2 through 4.

8 Then repeat step 5, but this time make sure that the point of the heart is pointing toward the last bead you have strung (a 6-mm rose quartz bead). You are starting the second side of the necklace, so be aware of the direction the heart beads are pointing so that both sides mirror each other.

9 Continue to create the other side of the necklace by repeating steps 2 through 5 three times. You should end here with a 4-mm crystal bead.

10 Now string on your last three 8-mm rose quartz beads.

11 Finish off the beading cord with another **bead tip**.

12 Use flat-nosed pliers to open your jump ring, and then close it around the loop on the arrow part of your toggle clasp.

13 Next use round-nosed pliers to curl the hook on the end of your bead tip around the jump ring that is now attached to the arrow side of the toggle. If necessary, finish closing the hook using flat-nosed pliers to ensure that the clasp is securely attached to the bead tip.

14 Use round-nosed pliers again to attach the heart-shaped side of the toggle to the other bead tip.

jeweler's tip

Because there are so many different shapes of stone beads available, the variation possibilities for this design are endless. Hematite is one stone that is often available in various shapes, but there are many other stones that are carved into shapes as well, such as rose quartz, black onyx, leopardskin jasper, and aventurine. One important detail to be aware of when working with shaped stone beads, especially on strung items like necklaces, is that some shapes have a definite top and bottom to them. Therefore, when you are assembling a jewelry piece you need to consider the orientation of the bead when the piece will be finished. This requires a little thinking ahead, but it can make a big difference in your completed jewelry design.

⬆ **variation**

Carnelian ranges in color from bright orange to dark burgundy. It is a stone of peace, believed to bring the wearer harmony. Hematite is an iron ore, so it is a hard stone and excellent for carving. Therefore, it can be purchased in a variety of bead shapes such as stars, hearts, moons, cubes, rice, teardrops, triangles, and tubes. Carnelian and hematite are combined for this variation. Carnelian beads (4 mm, 6 mm, and 8 mm) are mixed with hematite star-shaped and hematite rice-shaped beads. Sections of this necklace were knotted. The toggle closure is a whimsical teapot and spoon.

○ **gem folklore**

Rose quartz is a member of the quartz family. Other types of quartz include amethyst, citrine, and topaz. Quartz stones have historical and symbolic significance. The Aztecs used quartz to carve images such as skulls, which may have represented death and the afterlife. Quartz was also used in Asia to show honor to the gods. The Chinese emperor Wu required the doors of religious buildings be made of rock crystal, allowing bright light to illuminate the rooms within.

wisdom

With knowledge and understanding comes wisdom, a powerful attribute for anyone, whether you are an educated scholar or just a sensible individual. Few can dispute the need for insight and good judgment to help guide you through life. Perhaps that is why so many gemstones have a connection to wisdom. Fluorite, aventurine, rhodonite, sodalite, tiger's-eye, malachite, and quartz crystal are all stones associated with intelligence, insight, and diplomacy. They work with the conscious mind to bring the wearer of these gemstones truth and knowledge.

Sorcerers, magicians, magus, and high priests are all titles given to men of wisdom. The titles vary depending on the time period and culture. However, they all studied and believed in the powers of stones. In fact, like medical doctors of today who write prescriptions for drugs, wise men of the past dispensed their remedies via stone talismans that were believed to protect and heal the wearer.

In this chapter, each project utilizes gemstones that are connected to the attributes of wisdom. As with most gemstones, the stones related to wisdom were eventually appreciated for their beauty as well as their supposed powers. Therefore, we no longer create jewelry primarily as talismans but for the simple pleasure of wearing it and feeling good about ourselves. Maybe that is the secret to finding our own wisdom within.

fabulous fluorite bracelet

Fluorite has always been a fashionable gemstone because of its combination of colors. **Most commonly the colors of this stone include a mixture of greens, purples, and creams**, and it is very popular among gemstone jewelry lovers. However, it is also available in colors of yellow, pink, red, blue, and black. It is called fluorite because it contains hydrocarbons, which make it brightly fluorescent in ultraviolet light. Egyptian priests used this attribute to dazzle their followers. It is found in many countries, such as England and Switzerland, but the largest deposits are located in the United States. Gemstone legends associate fluorite with the conscious mind, **enriching the wearer's objective thoughts in order to make him think analytically** and thus minimize his emotional link to situations.

materials

- two 3-mm end cap beads
- sixteen 4-mm amethyst-colored bi-cone crystal beads
- five 6-mm square tanzanite-colored crystal beads
- thirty 6-mm fluorite beads
- bracelet-size memory wire
- heavy-duty wire cutters or memory wire shears
- jeweler's cement

step by step

1 Uncoil two loops of memory wire, and use heavy-duty wire cutters (or memory wire shears) to snip.

2 Glue one bead cap onto one end of the memory wire and set this aside to dry for 24 hours. Resist the urge to continue until you are sure your glue is dry and your bead cap is secure. Otherwise, your beads will slide right off your memory wire, and you will have to glue your cap on again.

3 Once the bead cap is secure, you can start threading the beads onto the memory wire. Begin with one 4-mm amethyst-colored crystal bead, and push it down the wire until it is up against the bead cap.

4 Now add three fluorite beads onto your wire, and slide those down also.

5 Next, you are ready to add on the crystal beads in a pattern that will be referred to as the "crystal bead station." It consists of one 4-mm amethyst-colored crystal, one 6-mm square tanzanite-colored crystal, and one 4-mm amethyst-colored crystal.

6 The next pattern will be referred to as the "fluorite bead station," and it is as follows: three fluorite beads, one 4-mm amethyst-colored crystal, and three fluorite beads.

7 You are now ready to alternate the bead station patterns on the remaining memory wire starting with the crystal bead station and following with the fluorite bead station. Continue to alternate stations until you have added four crystal and three fluorite bead stations.

8 Finish your bead stringing with three more fluorite beads and one 4-mm amethyst-colored crystal bead.

9 Now use your cutters or shears to cut any excess memory wire so that you have only ⅛" (3 mm) of wire left after your last bead.

10 Glue on your other bead cap, and carefully set your bracelet aside to dry for another 24 hours. When the glue is dry, your bracelet is ready to wear.

jeweler's tip

Memory wire has a lot of advantages. No clasp is needed, making it a easier to work with and to wear. One size fits all with this type of bracelet; since the average length of an adult bracelet can range from 6" to 9" (15 cm to 23 cm), this looping design alleviates the problem of whether or not a bracelet will fit.

The spring form of memory wire can be difficult to handle because it has so much movement to it. Be careful not to overstretch the wire by pulling on it or handling it too roughly. Once it stretches, it does not go back to its original size. In fact, the name "memory wire" comes from the fact that as you wear the wire, especially with the bracelet size, it will eventually stretch a little and conform to your body. Therefore, if you make a memory wire bracelet, it will "remember" your wrist.

⌃ variation

In this project variation, bright red glass beads separate 6-mm round and heart shaped hematite beads. Instead of finishing the ends of the bracelet with bead caps, round-nosed pliers were used to curl the ends. Then hematite heart beads and head pins were used to create dangles using the **wrap loop** technique, and they were added to each curled end of the bracelet.

◯ gem folklore

Hematite is sometimes referred to as bloodstone because the dust and powder that result from cutting this stone are a red color. The color also hints to the origin of its name, which originates from the Greek word for blood, *haima*. Hematite is a very hard stone because it is actually an iron ore. The powers connected to hematite include healing, alertness, and passion. Documentation of these powers dates back to 63 BC in a dissertation written for the King of Pontus, Mithridates the Great. The author, Azchalias of Babylon, wrote about the noble nature of hematite, which included assistance with legal issues as well as power over the wearer's destiny.

ice is nice lariat

The longer your lariat, the more ways you can wear it. This lariat is long enough so you can fold it in half, drape it around your neck, and then bring both ends through the center of the necklace. The combination of sterling silver wire, two sterling silver heart beads, **large white freshwater pearls, and icy-green aventurine** give this popular design a traditional look. Aventurine is a type of quartzite that contains mica, which creates the distinctive color. Though it is primarily found in India, it is also mined in Australia, Brazil, and Germany. Energies connected to aventurine include **increased intelligence and creativity, and it also protects the wearer against theft.** White pearls symbolize purity and have the powers of love, money, and luck.

materials

- twenty-eight 6-mm white oval freshwater pearls
- twenty-seven 6-mm aventurine beads
- 2 sterling heart beads
- two 2" (5 cm) head pins
- 10' (30 m) of 24-gauge (.50 mm) wire
- flush-cut wire cutters
- round-nosed pliers
- flat-nosed pliers
- jeweler's file
- polishing cloth
- nylon-nosed pliers

step by step

1 Begin by cutting approximately 12" (30 cm) of 24-gauge wire, and wipe the wire with a polishing cloth by putting the cloth in one hand and pulling the piece of wire through the cloth with the other hand.

2 Use the **wrap loop** technique to make a wrap loop on one end of the wire.

3 Slide one pearl onto your wire, and push it up against the wrap made in the previous step.

4 Create another wrap loop so that the wrap is up against the pearl bead, and trim off excess wire.

5 Take your remaining wire, and use the **wrap loop** technique again to connect it to one of the loops on the pearl piece made in steps 2 through 4. Don't forget to connect the loops of wire before closing the wrap.

6 Slide one aventurine bead onto your wire, and push it up against the wrap made in the previous step.

7 Again, add another wrap loop on the other end of your aventurine bead.

8 Continue this process of alternating pearl and aventurine beads and connecting wrap loops until you have used all of your beads, ending with a pearl bead. You should have approximately 40" (102 cm) of beaded chain made. When you run out of your first 12" (30 cm) of wire, just cut another 12" (30 cm) and proceed. If your wire becomes bent or kinked, use your nylon-nosed pliers and pull the wire through the jaws of the pliers in order to straighten it.

9 Now slide one of your sterling heart beads onto a 2" (5 cm) head pin.

10 Use the **wrap loop** technique to connect the head pin to one end of the beaded chain you completed in step 8.

11 Repeat steps 9 and 10 to add the second heart bead to the other end of your chain.

12 Finally, double check your wire wraps to make sure none are poking out. If they are, use your jeweler's file to smooth rough areas so that these don't scratch the wearer.

jeweler's tip

When using the **wrap loop** technique to create long chains, instead of cutting a number of small wire pieces for each loop you will create, it is helpful to work with one long piece of wire and create many loops from this piece. Work with pieces of wire that are about 12" (30 cm) in length for easier handling and to reduce the amount of scrap wire generated.

If your wire has become tarnished before you are ready to use it, wipe the pieces of wire with a soft polishing cloth a few times before starting to wrap. A pair of nylon-nosed pliers is also helpful for straightening your wire since it can become bent and kinked as you work.

gem folklore

Since the darker shades of green aventurine are considered more valuable than the lighter shades (which are sometimes even gray in color) it is not unusual that this stone is often dyed. In fact, naturally occurring dark green aventurine is thought to be so valuable that it is almost as rare is real jade, and like jade, aventurine is used in carvings as well as jewelry. Besides stone carvers and jewelry makers, gamblers also find this to be an important stone since talismans made from aventurine are associated with money and luck.

variation

In contrast to the icy look of the white pearl and aventurine lariat, Kate Ferrant Richbourg used the same wire technique to create this variation. The mixture of pearls, crystals, and metal beads in shades of gray give this lariat a feeling of richness and opulence. In addition, a variety of bead shapes were included, such as oval, square, diamond, rectangular, and round. Kate also chose to include an assortment of beads as tassels for both ends of the lariat. Each bead on the tassel is a separate dangle created by using head pins for the beads and she attached them to each other using wrap loops.

sweet sugilite earrings

Stone beads are available in a variety of shapes. Therefore, by simply using different shapes of beads such as hearts or squares, you can add a different dimension to your jewelry designs. The heart-shaped beads used in these earrings are made of **sugilite, which is actually a mineral, not a gemstone.** Though the largest deposits come from South Africa, the name of this mineral originated from Ken-ichi Sugi, a Japanese geologist who discovered it in 1944.

Colors of sugilite include purple, brown, yellow, pink, and black. However, the purple sugilite is most often used in jewelry designs. **Even though this mineral was discovered during the twentieth century, the powers of strength, safety, healing, and wisdom** have been attributed to it. Pearls and crystals are included as accents, along with sterling heart charms, on these very feminine earrings.

materials

- two 11 mm x 12 mm sugilite heart beads
- four 4-mm white pearl beads
- four 4-mm aurora borealis clear crystal beads
- 2 eurowire ear hooks
- two 2" (5-cm) eye pins
- two 16 mm x 16 mm heart charms
- round-nosed pliers
- flat-nosed pliers

step by step

1 Start by taking one of the eye pins and sliding on the beads in the following order: 1 pearl, 1 crystal, 1 heart, 1 crystal, and 1 pearl.

2 Then use round- and flat-nosed pliers to create a **wrap loop** on the end of the eye pin, making sure to slip on the ear hook before closing the wrap.

3 Now use your round-nosed pliers to open the eye on your eye pin.

4 Take your heart charm and slip it onto the open eye.

5 Next, close the eye again using your round-nosed pliers. If necessary, use flat-nosed pliers to close up the eye, but make sure you do not flatten the eye. You want to make sure that your charm can still move back and forth once attached to the eye pin.

6 Repeat all the above steps to make another earring so that you have a matching pair.

jeweler's tip

One of the advantages to using stone beads that have been cut into shapes, such as the sugilite heart beads or onyx square beads in these projects, is that they can also be used alone as a pendant. You can do this by simply adding one of the sugilite hearts to a head pin and using the **wrap loop** technique to create a loop at the top. Then add this pendant to a beaded necklace or even a silver chain. Stone shapes also allow for super quick earrings. With two stone shaped beads, two head pins, and two ear hooks, you can whip up a pretty pair of earrings in just a few minutes.

gem folklore

Natural sugilite, though beautiful, can be a little expensive, running anywhere from $30 to hundreds of dollars for a strand of beads, depending on their size and quality. This has made the use of synthetic sugilite very popular. While some jewelry makers cringe at the thought of using synthetic material in their jewelry, it is really a personal choice, which can depend on a number of variables. If you are determined to use only natural sugilite, a little can go a long way. It can be used as accents to other beads, or one large bead can be used as the focal point of a jewelry piece.

⌃ variation　Geometric shapes in this earring variation create a modern, rather than romantic, style. The black onyx beads are square-shaped, but the bead holes were drilled diagonally through the squares. Bright fuchsia-colored crystal beads add a source of bright color to each earring above the sterling, swirl dangle. Though the sterling swirls were purchased, they can be easily created using a few inches of round sterling silver wire and a pair of round-nosed and nylon-nosed pliers. (It may take a little practice to ensure that the swirls are symmetrical.) Onyx is often used in jewelry designs. It is believed to bring the wearer strength and is also considered a protective stone.

tin cup necklace

Rhodonite is a pink stone with streaks and swirls of gray and black throughout and has the **power to give the wearer calm, coherent thoughts. Other powers associated with this stone include self-confidence and clarity.** It is found around the globe. However, some of the largest deposits are located in Sweden, Britain, Russia, India, North America, South Africa, and Australia.

Rhona Farber combined rhodonite with large gray pearls in this once trendy now classic "tin cup" necklace design. Gray nylon beading thread connects the stations of beads and color-coordinates with the pearls and crystals. **Bright pink crystals provide a contrast to the other cool colors used in this piece.** The finished necklace measures approximately 16" (41 cm) and includes an unusual square-shaped toggle decorated with a flower design.

materials

- five 8-mm rhodonite beads
- four 8-mm gray pearls
- ten 4-mm gray crystal beads
- eight 4-mm bright pink crystal beads
- 2 bead tips
- one #4 gray nylon cord

- with needle
- scissors
- instant glue or jeweler's cement
- ruler
- round-nosed pliers
- flat-nosed pliers
- awl or Tri-Cord Knotter

step by step

1 Start by attaching a **bead tip** to one end of your nylon cord.

2 Now tie an overhand knot on your cord 1" (3 cm) away from the bead tip.

3 Then slip on one gray crystal bead, one rhodonite bead, and another gray crystal bead onto your cord, and push these beads up against your knot.

4 Using either **traditional knotting** or the **Tri-Cord Knotter**, tie another knot, and push it up against the last bead strung. At this point, you have created one bead station.

5 Repeat steps 2 through 4, but this time, substitute pink crystal beads for the gray crystal beads and substitute a gray pearl bead for the rhodonite bead.

6 Continue to add these bead stations, alternating with five rhodonite stations and four pearl stations until you have a total of nine stations.

7 Measure 1" (3 cm) away from your last station, and attach your second **bead tip**.

8 Finish off your tin cup necklace with a toggle clasp by using round-nosed pliers to curl the bead tip hooks around the loop of each toggle section.

jeweler's tip

After making your tin cup necklace, you may notice some bends or kinks in your cord, especially if you use the type of cord that comes wrapped on a card with an attached needle. To remove the kinks, simple hang your necklace up on a hook or door knob. Gravity will soon straighten the cord. When storing tin cup–style pieces, it is recommended that you also hang them up. Otherwise, the cord can become tangled, causing unwanted knots.

A similar tin cup look can be accomplished by using colored beading wire, which is available in a variety of colors. Instead of knotting between bead stations, use crimp beads to secure the beads in stations onto the wire.

gem folklore

Tiger's-eye possesses the powers of courage, energy, and luck. Its name may have come from the stripes of black and yellow that characterize the stone; they are actually fibrous minerals. This combination of colors from light to dark is referred to as chatoyant. While tiger's-eye is the brown and yellow variety of this gemstone, which is part of the quartz family, there are other varieties: cat's-eye is green and gray; hawk's eye is gray and blue; and bull's-eye or ox-eye is the color of dark mahogany.

⌃ variation

While the tin cup design is a classic, there are a number of variations possible. For the necklace pictured, two strands of beading cord were knotted together and enclosed in one **bead tip**. Bead stations of rose quartz hearts, 8-mm tiger's-eye beads, and pink crystal beads were alternately placed every few inches (5 cm to 8 cm) on the cord. A heart-shaped toggle clasp reinforces the heart theme of this necklace.

strength

Strength involves being physically strong and mentally strong. Many gemstones, including hematite, howlite, onyx, sugilite, and lapis, are connected to attributes associated with strength. Powers such as courage, self-control, self-expression, and energy invigorate the body and soul. Myths surrounding the powers associated with stones are rich with details about how stones can make you strong. Ancient Roman soldiers often wore stone talismans for protection while in battle. Warriors attached pieces of stone to their weapons to ensure accuracy, and men of thought used some stones to help fortify their powers of concentration. While ancient peoples used stones to protect and enhance might, eventually, these stones of strength were incorporated into jewelry used for body ornamentation.

Today, gemstones are used primarily for adornment. However, stone folklore still influences many modern jewelry designers, thus inspiring them to include these powerful gemstones in their hand-crafted jewelry. By combining old ideas with new functions, you can make a connection between the past and the future through your own gemstone bead creations and feel the power of creativity by making a piece of jewelry you can wear and enjoy.

The projects in this chapter have been developed to include these stones of power and strength. While you may not need a stone to help you through a battle, wearing a stone of power might help reinforce your own personal strengths.

dangle beaded choker

Hematite is an iron ore, so this mineral is heavier than most stone beads. The name originated from the Greek root *aima* or *ema*, meaning blood. When cut or deeply scratched, the powder from hematite is red in color. This stone is found in North America, South America, Italy, Britain, Germany, and Spain. **The powers associated with hematite include courage, self-control, concentration, and self-confidence.**

Hematite makes the wearer alert and acts as an aphrodisiac. The steely gray color of hematite is paired in this necklace with howlite, which is white with streaks of gray. **Howlite enhances creativity, artistic vision, and beauty.** This stone is found mainly in California and Nova Scotia. Memory wire is used as the stringing medium for this choker-length necklace. The contrasting creamy white and metal gray colors give this finished piece a modern and even a techno-trendy style.

materials

- 1½ coils of necklace-size memory wire
- one 22-gauge (.65 mm) 2" (5 cm) head pin
- eight 8-mm howlite beads
- three 20-mm howlite stone circle beads
- three 6-mm hematite beads
- eighty 4-mm hematite beads
- one 6-mm x 16-mm hematite teardrop bead
- two 3-mm end cap beads
- 3" (8 cm) of 22-gauge (.65mm) wire
- instant glue or jeweler's cement
- heavy-duty wire cutters or memory wire shears
- round-nosed pliers
- flat-nosed pliers
- jeweler's file
- ruler

step by step

1 First, add some glue to one end of your memory wire and attach one end-cap bead. Let it dry according to the manufacturer's instructions. It is important to make sure the glue is completely dry before continuing so that the beads do not slip off the wire while you are working.

2 While the glue is drying, you can make the center dangle. Start by using a jeweler's file to smooth both ends of your 3" (8 cm) piece of 22-gauge wire.

3 Use round-nosed and flat-nosed pliers to create a **wrap loop** on one end of the wire so that there is approximately 2" (5 cm) of wire left on the end.

4 Put one 6-mm hematite bead inside of one of the howlite stone circle beads, line up the holes in both the hematite and circle beads, and then slip the wire through the beads.

5 Add another **wrap loop** to the end of the wire.

6 Now take your head pin and slip on one hematite teardrop bead.

7 Start a **wrap loop** on the end of the head pin, but before you wrap the head pin around itself, slip it onto the end loop created in step 5. Then complete the wrapping. This will complete the dangle part of your necklace. Set this piece aside for later.

8 After your bead cap is dry on your memory wire (which could take up to 24 hours), string on eight 4-mm hematite beads and one 8-mm howlite bead.

9 Repeat step 8 twice, and then add eight more 4-mm hematite beads.

10 Now put one 6-mm hematite bead inside of one of the howlite stone circle beads, line up the holes in both beads, and then slip them onto the memory wire. Push these down the wire gently (without stretching out the wire too much) until they are up against the beads previously added.

11 Repeat step 8 again, and then slide on the dangle you made in steps 2 through 7.

12 String on one 8-mm howlite bead, eight 4-mm hematite beads, and then repeat step 10 to add the hematite and circle bead.

13 Again, repeat the pattern in step 8 three times, and then string on eight 4-mm hematite beads.

14 At this point, make sure there are no gaps between any of the beads, and if necessary, gently push the beads down the wire so they are up against each other.

15 Finally, carefully cut excess memory wire using heavy-duty wire cutters so that about ⅛" (3 mm) of wire is left at the end. (Be careful when cutting memory wire because it has a tendency to fly away when cut.)

16 Repeat the gluing procedure described in step 1, and again, make sure you let the glue completely dry before handling your finished necklace or the beads will slide off.

jeweler's tip

Memory wire is available in necklace, bracelet, and ring size, so you could make a matching set. One advantage to using memory wire is that no clasps are necessary, and one size fits all. Memory wire is also excellent for beginners and even children to use. Just make sure an adult is there to cut the wire.

When you are cutting memory wire, use heavy-duty wire cutters or memory wire shears. The wire is extremely thick, so don't use your good wire cutters that you normally would use for thinner gauge wire; they will be damaged.

◆ variation

Instead of hematite and howlite, this dangle necklace is primarily made of unakite stone beads with accents of leopardskin jasper and silver-colored, glass spacer beads. The unakite beads are a mixture of 8-mm and 4-mm round beads and oval beads. The leopardskin jasper beads include 6-mm and 8-mm round beads, ovals, one teardrop, and three heart-shaped beads. The glass beads add some sparkle to the earth tones in the stone beads. Unakite is a balancing stone that encourages love, while jasper is a healing stone once used in ancient rain ceremonies. Bead caps finish both ends of this memory wire necklace.

○ gem folklore

Hematite and howlite are both very popular stones because they are economical and very versatile. Due to its shiny, neutral gray color, hematite looks great with all kinds of other stones. When working with this stone, use a strong stringing medium. Memory wire, tiger-tail, or beading wire all work well, but hematite can eventually cut through monofilament, nylon, or silk. The powers associated with hematite include courage, self-control, concentration, and self-confidence.

Naturally colored howlite also pairs well with a variety of other stones. It is often dyed to look like more expensive semiprecious stones such as lapis and turquoise. Bead suppliers will normally use terms like "turquoise howlite" and "lapis howlite" to indicate that the stone is really dyed howlite. While many stones are heat treated and often dyed to enhance color, dyed howlite can eventually fade and rub off. So, keep this in mind when selecting stones for your project.

bottomless sandals

Kick off your shoes and adorn your feet with gemstone beads and sterling silver chain. On one end of the chain is a loop, which you connect to your second toe. The rest of the sandal, consisting of beads and chain, rests against the top of your foot and then wraps around your ankle. A hook secures the sandals to your foot. While this project was made to fit an average, women's size 7 foot, you can make larger or smaller sizes of sandals by adjusting the length of chain. With these Bottomless Sandals, you not only enjoy the freedom of bare feet, you can create your own unique style of fun. Malachite triangles and square onyx beads are used in this project to connect the chain. **Malachite is associated with leadership abilities** and is often worn by travelers as a guardian stone. **Onyx protects the wearer and was worn in ancient times to assist those in battle.**

materials

- eight 8-mm x 8-mm malachite triangle beads
- six 4-mm x 6-mm black onyx square beads
- 20" (51 cm) of medium link sterling silver chain
- 6" (15 cm) of 20-gauge (.80 mm) wire
- approximately 40" (102 cm) of 22-gauge (.65 mm) wire
- jeweler's file
- round-nosed pliers
- flat-nosed pliers
- wire cutters
- ruler

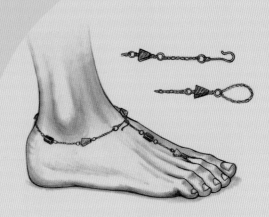

step by step

1 Begin constructing the first sandal by using wire cutters to cut seven 1" (3 cm) pieces of chain and one 3" (8 cm) piece of chain.

2 With 22-gauge wire, use the wrap loop technique to start a **wrap loop**, but before wrapping the wire around itself, insert the last links from the two ends of the 3" (8 cm) piece of chain into the loop.

3 After finishing the wrap above, slip on one malachite triangle bead with the pointed end toward the wrap.

4 Create another **wrap loop** on the opposite end of the wire, and before finishing the wrapping of the wire, slip on the last link of one of the 1" (3 cm) pieces of chain previously cut.

5 Connect a **wrap loop** of 22-gauge wire onto the last link of the 1" (3 cm) piece of chain used in the step above.

6 Slip a black onyx square bead onto the wire.

7 Create another **wrap loop** on the opposite end of the wire, and before finishing the wrapping of the wire, slip on the last link of one of the 1" (3 cm) pieces of chain previously cut.

8 Continue to connect beads and chain alternating between the malachite triangle beads and black onyx square beads until you have connected a total of three triangle and three square beads. Make sure that you do not finish the wrap loop after slipping on the last square bead.

9 After the last square bead, connect another 1" (3 cm) piece of chain, finish wrapping the wire loop, and then slip on one malachite triangle. Make sure that the triangle is pointed in the opposite direction from the other triangles. (This will make more sense once you put your sandal on your foot.)

10 Again, create another **wrap loop** after your last triangle bead, and slip on your last piece of 1" (3 cm) chain before you finish wrapping the loop.

11 To complete the first sandal, use 20-gauge wire to create a **hook with wrap**.

12 Wrap the end of the **hook with wrap** around the last link in the chain piece added in step 10.

13 To ensure that the wire does not scratch your bare foot, use a **jeweler's file** to go back and file each looped area as well as the **hook with wrap**. This is very important since you will be walking around in these sandals and this movement could cause discomfort if any wire areas are not smooth.

14 Finally, repeat all the steps above to make another sandal so that you have a matching pair.

jeweler's tip

You can create different sizes of these sandals by simply changing the length of the finished piece. One way to determine how long your finished sandal should be is to use a tape measure. Wrap one end around your second toe and the rest down your foot and around your ankle to simulate the finished sandal. This measurement can help you determine how long each sandal should be. Remember that you will want to be able to walk around in these. So, do not make the finished sandal too tight. You want it to be a little loose, especially the part of the sandal that will stretch across the top of your foot.

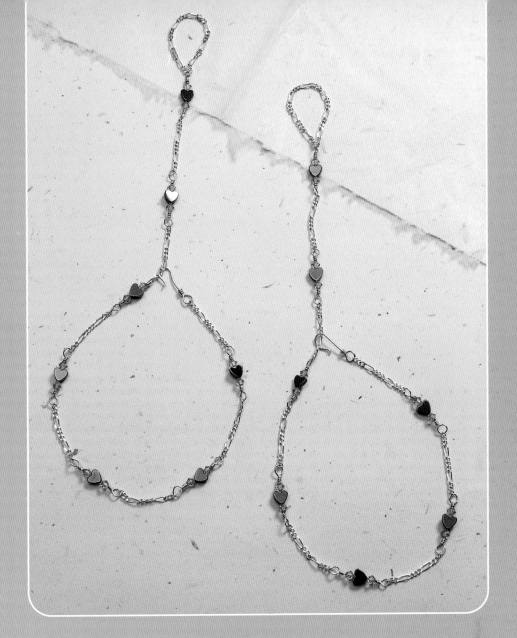

⬡ variation

Just like beads, chain is available in a variety of designs. This project variation uses a figaro style of chain instead of a simple cable chain. The figaro design alternates with three small links and one long oval link. Heart-shaped hematite beads are accented with 4-mm pink crystal beads for a more feminine look. Hematite makes the wearer alert and improves concentration and self control.

⬡ gem folklore

Malachite may break into pieces when danger approaches and is often associated with salesmen because it brings luck and protects travelers. Perhaps this myth arose because this copper ore is brittle. It takes true skill to carve and cut this stone. Because of this, some malachite may be treated to make it sturdier, or it may even be simulated. However, it is still very easy to find good-quality, naturally occurring malachite gemstones.

Naturally occurring onyx is also readily available, but it is not solid black. In fact, its colors vary from streaks of gray and white to streaks of black and white. However, when used in jewelry, it is often dyed black, and less often it is dyed green or blue. It is a very hard stone and is used for carvings as well as jewelry, which may be why it was once carved with symbols and worn as protective talismans.

chunky charm bracelet

Earthy green turquoise combined with sterling silver beads and theme charms give this bold bracelet a southwestern flare. It is **truly a statement piece, designed to be noticed by others and enjoyed by the wearer.** Sterling silver charms, including a pueblo house, sun face, and flute-playing Kokopelli, are evenly spaced throughout the bracelet so they dangle freely. Ornate tube-shaped beads decorate each end while smaller sterling silver daisies are spaced between various stone beads as accents.

The piece is finished off with a large toggle clasp. Turquoise used in this bracelet is primarily a dark green, but the beads also include a swirling mixture of blacks and browns. While most often associated with Native Americans because large quantities are found in North America, **turquoise is found in Central America, the Middle East, and around the world.** The Aztecs as well as the Egyptians used this stone for decorative purposes.

materials

- twelve 10-mm turquoise beads
- 8 sterling silver daisy spacer beads
- 2 sterling silver spiral tube beads, ¼" (5 mm) long
- one 21 mm x 24 mm sterling sun face charm
- one 19 mm x 12 mm sterling Kokopelli charm
- one 17 mm x 18 mm sterling pueblo house charm
- 1 sterling silver toggle clasp
- 2 sterling silver crimp beads
- approximately 10" (25 cm) of beading wire
- crimping pliers
- wire cutters

step by step

1 Start by taking either end of your toggle clasp and inserting one end of your beading wire through the loop or jump ring of the clasp (some toggles have jump rings connected and some do not).

2 Use a **crimp bead** and crimping pliers to secure the toggle piece to one end of the beading wire.

3 Slip on one daisy bead and one turquoise bead, making sure that both ends of the wire are inserted through the holes in the beads.

4 Use wire cutters to trim off the shorter end of the beading wire if necessary.

5 Then, on the longer end of beading wire, string on a spiral tube bead, turquoise bead, daisy bead, and another turquoise bead.

6 Add your pueblo house charm, and continue to string on three turquoise beads alternating with two daisy beads (turquoise, daisy, turquoise, daisy, turquoise).

7 At this point you are in about the middle of your bracelet. Slide on the sun face charm. If your charms have a definite front and back to them, make sure that you are aware of this when you add them to your bracelet so that they are all facing in the same direction.

8 Again, continue to string on three turquoise beads alternating with two daisy beads.

9 Next, add the Kokopelli charm, and finish stringing with one turquoise, one daisy, one turquoise, one spiral tube, one turquoise, and finally one daisy bead.

10 Slip the second **crimp bead** and the other end of the toggle clasp onto your beading wire.

11 Insert the wire back down through the crimp bead and last daisy and turquoise beads.

12 Use crimping pliers to secure the **crimp bead**, and use wire cutters to carefully trim off any excess beading wire.

jeweler's tip

When looking for charms to add to jewelry pieces, make sure they come with a jump ring, preferably one that is soldered closed. While you can create your own jump rings, most quality charm suppliers should provide jump rings with their charms.

With large beaded bracelets, anywhere from 8 mm up in size, you will often need to make the bracelet larger to accommodate for the diameter of the beads. So even though you may normally wear a 7" (18 cm) bracelet, if you are using large beads, you will need to make the bracelet ½" to 1" (1 cm to 3 cm) longer.

⌃ variation

Pearls and amethysts make up this variation design. Amethyst is a very popular semi-precious stone and makes the wearer gentle and amiable. Pearls add a classic touch and possess powers associated with love, protection, and luck. Though charms were left off and larger beads were used to create this bracelet variation, the basic stringing technique is the same. The large amethyst nugget beads are roughly faceted but highly polished. The spacer beads include small button pearl beads and purple crystal beads, which separate the chunky amethyst beads. A heart-shaped sterling silver toggle clasp finishes off this bracelet.

○ gem folklore

The name "turquoise" is believed to originate from the Turks who transported it from the Mediterranean to Europe. Today it is still mined primarily in parts of North America, including Nevada, New Mexico, Arizona, and California. Turquoise is a porous stone, so it should not be exposed to chemicals or even water. The colors of this stone range from blues to greens. When selecting turquoise, be careful to determine that it really is turquoise and not a dyed substitute. Howlite and sodalite are sometimes dyed to simulate the look of turquoise. Much of the turquoise available today is treated. Though it is not impossible to find high grades of turquoise, it can be costly. Lower grades of turquoise are sometimes waxed to enhance the color or to reduce porosity, making it suitable for jewelry.

dual-duet necklace

Crossing the line between function and form, **you can wear this double-strand necklace three ways.** First, keep both strands of beads attached to the large "S" hook and wear them together for a chunky, modern look. Your other two options are to remove one strand of beads from the hook and wear the remaining strand separately: the lemon chrysoprase with sterling silver daisy spacer beads or the turquoise nugget strand with a matching sterling silver and turquoise pendant. **Chrysoprase is a form of chalcedony and has been used for centuries by artisans for the purpose of ornamentation and sculpture** due to its hardness and brilliancy when polished.

materials

- 4 sterling silver bead tips
- 4 sterling silver jump rings
- 1 large "S" hook
- thirty-one 10-mm lemon chrysoprase beads
- 32 sterling silver daisy spacer beads

- thirty-nine 5-mm turquoise nugget beads
- 1 sterling silver and turquoise 20 mm x 15.8 mm bead
- one 2" (5-cm) 22-gauge (.65 mm) head pin
- 4' (1.2 m) of beading wire

- round-nosed pliers
- flat-nosed pliers
- wire cutters

step by step

1 First, cut a few feet of beading wire and attach a **bead tip** to one end of the wire.

2 Start by stringing on one daisy spacer bead and one chrysoprase bead, alternating until you have all of them strung on the beading wire.

3 Finish off this strand of beads with another **bead tip**.

4 Next, use the 20 mm x 15.8 mm sterling and turquoise bead to create a pendant by first slipping the bead onto a head pin.

5 Then, use round-nosed pliers and flat-nosed pliers to create a **wrap loop** on one end of the head pin, and set the pendant aside for later.

6 Take the rest of your beading wire and attach a **bead tip** to one end.

7 String on half of your turquoise bead nuggets, the sterling and turquoise pendant made previously in steps 4 and 5, and the rest of your turquoise beads.

8 Finish off this strand of beads with another **bead tip**.

9 Now slip one of your jump rings onto the hook of one of the bead tips, and use round-nosed pliers to curl the hook closed so that the jump ring is secure.

10 Repeat the previous step until each **bead tip** has a jump ring attached.

11 Finish off by attaching one jump ring from the strand of turquoise and one from the strand of chrysoprase to one side of the "S" hook and the other two ends of your bead strands to the opposite side of the "S" hook. Your strands should be positioned so that the larger chrysoprase bead strand is nested inside the turquoise strand.

● jeweler's tip

The design for this double strand necklace requires that one strand is nested inside of the other strand. To make sure that both fit together correctly, a bead board is especially useful. In addition, a hemostat, a surgical clamp available at most flea markets, is handy for clamping onto beading wire to ensure your beads do not slip off. Then before finishing the ends, you can check to see how the strands rest together. You could also make strands of equal length, then twist them together for a different look.

○ gem folklore

Native American myths surrounding the use of turquoise include using this stone to guard the dead and attaching turquoise to arrows to ensure accurate shots. While this stone's colors range from shades of greens to blues, the most sought after color of turquoise is sky blue. However, due to its popularity it is has become difficult to locate natural, blue turquoise that has not been treated by heat or chemicals.

Chrysoprase also has a number of myths related to it. During the Middle Ages, sorcerers carved this stone with magical symbols and used it in rituals. This stone is found in Germany, North America, and Brazil. The colors of this stone are most often found in shades of light greens and pale yellow.

⌃ variation

To make a more subtle necklace design, use earth-tone beads such as agate and black onyx and follow the assembly instructions for the main project. The 13 mm x 10 mm black lace agate beads are barrel shaped, and the different colors of the agate create enough contrast between the beads that there is no need for spacers. Instead, daisy spacers were used to break up the 4-mm strand of black onyx beads. Two 6-mm onyx beads were positioned in the middle of the strand to help secure the pendant, which was originally a bead. Agate provides protection and strength, while onyx is associated with energy.

peace

Peace is an often-elusive power searched for by cultures around the world. However, peace is not sought only by world leaders. Many of us seek peace or contentment within ourselves. When we try to calm our angry emotions, suppress our jealous natures, or distill our unreasonable fears, we are working toward the objective of inner peace. Serenity, harmony, and tranquility are all elements related to the idea of a peaceful nature, and by being at peace with ourselves, we can lead a happy and fulfilling life.

Making your own personal adornments using stones associated with harmony is one way to bring peace into your life. Numerous semi-precious stones, which are routinely incorporated in fine jewelry, are connected to the power of peace. Amethyst, for example, makes the wearer gentle, and citrine removes fear. Though neither is actually a crystallized stone, pearls and obsidian are also associated with the power of peace. Pearls come from oysters, so they are considered organic gems. Their believed powers and history date back far into Asian mythology. Obsidian is volcanic glass and was used by the Aztecs and Mayans to form tools and decorative objects. Other harmonious stones include malachite, carnelian, and peridot.

This chapter focuses on the power of peace, so the projects included use stones that have links to peace, tranquility, and harmony. Most first-time jewelry makers are surprised at the enjoyment they receive from making stone jewelry. Taking a handful of loose beads and arranging them in a pleasing design on your bead board is just the beginning. While you string each bead on your beading cord or connect each bead together using wire or chain, you will find the repetitive motion relaxing and calming as you sit and create jewelry art with your hands and your soul.

pearl power bracelet

Both trendy and classic, this pearl bracelet is strung with elastic cord so that it is easy to wear. There is no clasp to deal with since the bracelet can be easily slipped on over your hand. **The elastic cord updates this classic pearl bracelet that can be worn with a business suit or a pair of jeans.** A few crystal beads are included in the design to not only accent the pearls but to help hide the knot used to connect the cord. Since pearls are now available in a rainbow of colors, white is no longer the only choice for pearl lovers.

Pearls are very porous so they need a little extra care than most beads. When getting dressed, make sure you put on your makeup, hair spray, and perfume before you put on any pearl jewelry (the same goes for amber, by the way). For a gentle cleaning, wipe your pearl jewelry with a soft cloth or occasionally clean with mild soapy water. Never use jewelry solvents or ammonia-based cleaning solutions on them. Store in a jewelry box lined with felt or in a soft cloth pouch.

materials

- 10" (25 cm) 0.5-mm elastic jewelry cord
- twenty 8-mm gold-colored pearls
- four 6-mm rose-colored crystal beads
- scissors
- tape
- instant glue or jeweler's cement

step by step

1 Start by adding a piece of tape to one end of the elastic cord. This will prevent your beads from sliding off as you string them on.

2 String five pearl beads and one crystal bead on the cord. Repeat this pattern of five pearls and one crystal three more times. It is important that the last bead you string on is a crystal bead.

3 Now slide your beads into the middle of the elastic cord.

4 Using the two ends of the elastic cord, tightly tie a **square knot**.

5 Then, drop a small amount of instant glue or jeweler's cement onto your square knot, and use scissors to trim off excess cord. Do not worry about getting all the cord trimmed off. You do not want to cut too closely to your knot, and a tiny amount of cord left over will not be seen.

6 Now slide the crystal bead, which is next to your knot, over the knot that was glued in the previous step.

7 Allow glue try dry for at least a few hours or overnight, depending on the manufacturer's directions.

jeweler's tip

When making a bracelet using elastic cording, your finished piece should always be about 1" (3 cm) smaller than the bracelet size you normally wear because the elastic will stretch. The finished bracelet for this project is approximately 6" (15 cm), so it will fit someone who normally wears a 7" (18 cm) bracelet. If you normally wear a smaller or larger bracelet than 7" (18 cm), then you will need to adjust the measurements and bead quantities in the main project directions accordingly.

Also, when slipping on an elastic-style bracelet, be careful to not over-stretch it. For best results, put the bracelet over your fingers, and then push so that the beads roll over your hand. This will help prevent the elastic from stretching out prematurely. If you find yourself wearing this bracelet often, you may also want to consider restringing it every few months to ensure that the elastic keeps its integrity.

gem folklore

Pearls have been popular since ancient times. Dedicated by the Romans to Isis, they were worn to obtain her favor. Early Asian mythology claimed that pearls fell from the sky when dragons fought among the clouds. Hindu mythology tells a story of the goddess Maya, who created a pearl encrsuted tank of crystal that was so clear those who gazed upon it were tempted to dive in as if it were a pool of fresh water. Another Hindu legend tells of the Kapla tree, and from its branches hung pearls and emeralds. Powers of peace, love, protection, and luck are associated with cultured and freshwater pearls.

⌂ variation

D.D. Hess created her own variation of this pearl bracelet using elastic cording, Biwa-style pearls, 8-mm tiger's-eye beads, and lampwork beads. D.D. is a jewelry designer and glass artist, so she made the lampwork beads herself using glass rods from Italy and an oxygen and propane torch. She infused pieces of goldstone in her lampwork beads to create the sparkling swirls that bring out the gold-tone colors of the tiger's-eye beads.

exotic pearl earrings

Pearl jewelry doesn't have to be understated or monochromatic; it can also have an eclectic, ethnic style when combined with handcrafted beads from India and sparkling crystals. Talented metal artisans created the ornate sterling silver beads that give these pearl earrings an exotic flavor. **Connected to the powers of peace, love, luck, purity, and honesty,** pearls are a favorite component for many jewelry lovers.

They are considered organic gems because pearls are produced through biological methods. However, they are included in the category of precious and semiprecious stones due to their beauty and value as personal adornments. Today pearls are more affordable than ever, and they are available in a wide variety of shapes and colors.

materials

- 2 sterling silver eurowire ear hooks
- twelve 4-mm sterling daisy spacers
- two 5-mm gray pearl beads
- two 6-mm clear crystal beads
- two 4-mm white pearls beads
- two 8 mm x 6 mm sterling baroque dot beads
- two 2" (5 cm) 24-gauge (.50 mm) eye pins
- two 1" (3 cm) 24-gauge (.50 mm) head pins
- wire cutters
- round-nosed pliers
- flat-nosed pliers
- jeweler's file

step by step

1 Begin by stringing the following beads onto one of the sterling silver eye pins in this order: daisy bead, crystal bead, daisy bead, baroque bead, daisy bead, gray pearl bead, and daisy bead.

2 Add an ear hook onto the top of the eye pin by using the **wrap loop** technique, remembering to add the ear hook to the loop before wrapping it closed.

3 Set this part of the earring aside for later use.

4 Now it is time to make the second part of the earring. Add one daisy bead, one 4-mm white pearl bead, and one daisy bead onto a head pin.

5 Use the **wrap loop** technique to finish the top of the head pin so that the loop is close to the beads added in the previous step. The finished piece should be approximately ½" (1 cm) in length.

6 Trim the excess off the head pin using wire cutters.

7 If necessary, use a **jeweler's file** to smooth off the wrapped area around the head pin.

8 Now, pick up the first part of the earring, and use round-nosed pliers to slightly open the loop on the end of the eye pin.

9 Slip the loop of the second earring part onto the open eye of the pin.

10 Again, use round-nosed pliers to close the loop on the end of the eye pin.

11 Repeat all the steps above to make a second earring so that you have a matching pair.

jeweler's tip

Probably the most difficult part of making earrings is to make sure that both match, especially in length. But do not make yourself too crazy when trying to do this. Remember that though you may hold them up next to each other to see how they look after you have made them, you will be wearing them on either side of your head. Therefore, if one is a little longer than the other, it will not be noticeable. To ensure that earrings are the same length, first be aware of the length of head pins and wire as you use them. You may even want to use a ruler to measure each section as you work. Also, some people prefer to make earrings simultaneously rather than one at a time, which requires that each step of the process be immediately repeated. Experiment and find a method that works best for you.

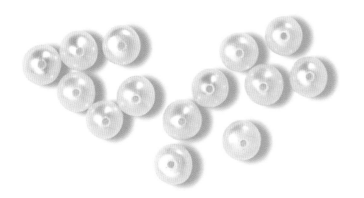

gem folklore

At one time, Japan was the world's largest producer of cultured pearls. Unfortunately, this all changed when a combination of water pollution, oyster viruses, and overcrowded harvests destroyed numerous pearl crops. China now manufactures the majority of freshwater pearls, and its methods have changed the pearl industry. Today, pearls are extremely affordable and are available in an unimaginable variety of colors and shapes. A genuine classic, the pearl has never been out of fashion and continues to grow in popularity.

◈ variation

Since pearls, crystals, and sterling silver beads come in a huge variety of designs and colors, there are a limitless number of variations possible. This variation includes sterling silver daisy beads; 3-mm pearls; sterling silver tube-shaped beads; amethyst-colored 4-mm crystals; and 8-mm gray "potato" pearl beads. Potato pearls are named after the vegetable because they have the same shape. Many of the larger freshwater pearls are available in this shape and come in a variety of colors ranging from neutral whites and grays to more brilliant purples and pinks.

pretty purple lariat

Amethyst, the bright purple stone included in this 32" (81 cm) chain-and-bead lariat, is an extremely popular type of quartz often used in fine jewelry. While this stone is mined in a number of countries, including the United States, Madagascar, and India, the largest mines, which also produce the best quality amethyst, are located in Brazil. **The darker the amethyst, the higher the value, so this stone is often treated to enhance its color.**

One reason lariats are so popular is because they are versatile. The lariat in this project is normally worn two different ways. First, because there is a loop of chain on one end and the bead drop on the other end, the end with the bead can be inserted through the chain loop, thus allowing you to wear this piece as a long necklace. The other style that works well with this design is a double choker style. By wrapping the chain twice around your neck and then dropping the beaded end down through the chain loop end in front, you can create a completely different style with the same piece of jewelry.

materials

- fifteen 8 mm x 6 mm oval amethyst beads
- thirty 4-mm aurora borealis clear crystal beads
- 20" (51 cm) of 2-mm figaro chain

- 30" (76 cm) of 24-gauge (.50 mm) wire
- one 2" (5 cm) 24-gauge (.50 mm) head pin
- flush-cut wire cutters

- round-nosed pliers
- flat-nosed pliers
- polishing cloth
- nylon-nosed pliers
- jeweler's file

step by step

1 To assemble this lariat, it's a good idea to start by cutting all the pieces of chain you will need. Begin by examining the chain. You will notice that figaro chain is made up of an alternate pattern of three small links and one large link.

2 Use your wire cutters to cut your first piece of chain so that it includes the following link pattern: 3 small, 1 large, 3 small, 1 large, and 3 small.

3 Repeat this process until you have 14 pieces of chain cut.

4 Now cut one piece of the figaro chain so that you have 11 units of the following pattern: 1 large oval link, 3 small links, 1 large oval link.

5 At this stage, you are ready to start connecting the chain, wire, and beads. Start by cutting approximately 12" (30 cm) of 24-gauge (.50 mm) wire, and wipe the wire with a polishing cloth.

6 Use the **wrap loop** technique to start a loop on one end of the wire, but do not wrap the loop closed yet.

7 Take one piece of chain you cut in step 4, and slip the large link on one end of the chain onto the wire loop.

8 Repeat this for the other end of that same piece of chain so that both ends of the chain are in the wrap loop.

9 Finish wrapping the wire loop closed.

10 Next slide on one crystal bead, one amethyst bead, and another crystal bead onto the wire, and push the beads up against the **wrap loop**.

11 Using the **wrap loop** technique again, start another loop, but do not wrap it closed yet.

12 Take one of the pieces of chain you cut in steps 2 and 3, and slide the first link on one end of the piece of chain (it will be one of the smaller links from the pattern) onto the wire loop.

13 Finish wrapping the wire loop closed.

14 Repeat the process of alternating a piece of chain with a wrap loop wire and bead section until you have used all 14 pieces of previously cut chain. When you run out of your 12" (30 cm) of wire, just cut another 12" (30 cm) piece and proceed. If your wire becomes kinked as you work with it, use your nylon-nosed pliers and pull the wire through the jaws of the pliers in order to straighten it.

15 Finally, to finish off the end of your lariat, slide one crystal bead, one amethyst bead, and one crystal bead onto your head pin.

16 Create another **wrap loop** on the end of the head pin, and slip the end of the last piece of chain you added onto the loop before wrapping it closed.

17 Though your lariat is finished at this point, it is a good idea to go back and check all the wrap loops to make sure no wire is poking out. If you find some rough areas, use a **jeweler's file** to file them smooth.

jeweler's tip

When working with silver wire and chain, invariably you will start to have some scraps piling up. Whatever you do, don't throw these away. Save them because eventually, believe it or not, you may be able to use them. Leftover chain links can be used as jump rings, and there are times you may just need one little piece of wire for something. That's when you reach into your bag or container of leftover silver scraps. Some jewelry-making suppliers will also buy your scrap silver or will provide exchanges for it.

⌃ variation

Turquoise and silver seem to be made for each other and are the components of this lariat variation and matching pair of earrings. The turquoise nuggets are 5 mm and each bead is accented with sterling silver daisy spacer beads. The beaded segments, which are connected together with figaro sterling silver chain, are strung on 22-gauge (.65 mm) sterling silver round wire. The **simple loop** technique, instead of the wrap loop, was used to attach the beaded segments to the chain. This 30" (76 cm) lariat is finished off with a hook on one end and a triple loop component on the other end, thus allowing it to be worn lots of different ways. Connect the hook and loop and wear it as a single-strand necklace. Wrap it around your neck two times to wear it as a choker. Or slip the hook into one of the larger chain links to wear as a lariat.

gem folklore

The popularity of amethyst is not a modern occurrence, as the color purple has always had strong symbolic meaning in many cultures. Believed to make the wearer gentle and amiable, amethyst was also thought by ancient peoples to protect one from drunkenness. In fact, its name comes from the Greek word *mèthystos*, which means "not drunken." Other mythological powers associated with this stone include dreaming, healing, peace, happiness, and protection.

carnelian and citrine y necklace

The Y necklace design was originally popular during the Victorian era and then came back into style during the latter part of the twentieth century. Now this design is considered a classic and is a staple jewelry item required in any jewelry wearer's collection. **Carnelian and citrine are combined in this updated version of the Y necklace design, and both gemstones are associated with the powers of peace.** Carnelian is a gemstone with a waxy luster. It is available in shades that range from bright orange to deep red. Believed to promote peace and harmony, ancient **Egyptians wore carnelian on their hands to calm emotions of anger, jealousy, envy, and hatred.** Citrine is a yellow form of quartz crystals. It removes fear and also ensures a good night's sleep because it prevents nightmares.

materials

- nineteen 6-mm carnelian beads
- ten 8 mm x 6 mm oval citrine beads
- one 2" (5 cm) head pin
- 24" (61 cm) of 22-gauge (.65 mm) wire
- 10" (25 cm) of medium link chain
- two 7-mm jump rings
- 1 "S" hook
- round-nosed pliers
- flat-nosed pliers
- flush-cut wire cutters
- polishing cloth
- nylon-nosed pliers
- jeweler's file

step by step

1 Start by using wire cutters to cut 8 pieces of sterling silver chain so that each section of chain includes 7 links. Your chain sections should be about 1" (3 cm) in length.

2 Now cut approximately 12" (30 cm) of 22-gauge (.65 mm) wire, and wipe the wire with a polishing cloth.

3 Use the **wrap loop** technique to start a loop on one end of the wire, but do not wrap the loop closed yet.

4 Take one of your jump rings, and slip it onto the loop you created in the previous step.

5 Finish wrapping the wire loop closed, and slip one carnelian bead, one citrine bead, and another carnelian bead onto your wire.

6 Push the beads up against the wrap loop.

7 Using the **wrap loop** technique again, start another loop, but do not wrap it closed yet.

8 Now take one of the pieces of chain you cut in step 1, slip one of the last links of the chain piece onto the loop, and finish wrapping your loop closed.

9 Continue to connect pieces of chain with the wrap-looped citrine and carnelian sections until you have used all but one piece of chain. You will probably use up the first piece of 22-gauge (.65 mm) wire that you cut, so use the wire you have left after cutting it in step 2. Again, use a polishing cloth to clean the wire, and if necessary, use nylon-nosed pliers to run the wire through if you have any kinks or bends you want to remove.

10 On the last carnelian and citrine bead and wire section, connect another jump ring onto the last loop that you wrap closed. At this point,

you should have 8 carnelian and citrine wire bead sections with 7 pieces of chain attaching them and jump rings attached to both ends.

11 Now you are ready to create the "Y" part of your Y necklace. Locate the center piece of chain on your wire and chain piece that you have made in the steps above.

12 Next, locate the center link in the center piece of chain. Since you had seven links in each piece of chain, you just need to count three links over from either side into the middle.

13 Make another **wrap loop**, and before wrapping the loop closed, slip the loop onto the center link you located in the step above.

14 Add one carnelian bead onto the wire, and begin another **wrap loop**.

15 Before wrapping the loop closed in the step above, take your last piece of chain that you cut in step 1, slip the last link of one end of the chain piece onto the loop, and finish wrapping your loop closed.

16 Next slide on one citrine bead, one carnelian bead, and another citrine bead onto the head pin.

17 You need to make another **wrap loop**, but this time, you make one on the end of the head pin, and again, slip on the last link of chain onto the loop before wrapping it closed.

18 To finish your Y necklace, slip both ends of the necklace that have the jump rings onto either end of your "S" hook.

19 Before wearing the necklace, double-check to make sure that the wire wrap areas are smooth. Use a **jeweler's file** to smooth any wire that is sticking out.

jeweler's tip

Though the basic design of this necklace is in the shape of a Y, there are still a number of variations possible. Of course, changing the type of beads or chain used is one obvious way to create a different look. However, you can also vary the length. Make it choker length, 15" to 16" (38 cm to 41 cm) for a trendy look, or add more chain and beads for a long, classy 30" (76 cm) or even 40" (102 cm) Y necklace. Also, remember that the middle dangle is the focal point of this design. While beads look great, charms are also an alternative to consider.

variation

Royal blue lapis lazuli beads are combined with sterling silver daisy spacer beads and Austrian crystal beads for this alternate Y necklace. A blue lampwork teardrop bead dangles from the center, and figaro rather than link chain was used to connect the bead and wire sections. Also, instead of a purchased "S" style clasp, this necklace has a **figure eight eye** and **hook with**

wrap. The dominant stone used in this necklace, lapis lazuli, is made up of a number of minerals including lazurite, calcite, and pyrite. The pyrite in lapis can be seen in gray metallic veins that sparkle throughout the stone. Lapis assists the wearer with strength of character and purity of heart. It also has the power of courage.

gem folklore

As one of the many forms of quartz, citrine is a common mineral that comes in a wide range of colors. However, the yellow form of this quartz, citrine, is still considered a semiprecious stone, even though it is not uncommon. It is one of the birth stones for the month of November and is an anniversary stone for the ninth year of marriage.

One of the most prevalent myths surrounding citrine is the idea that it helps facilitate sleep; however, it also promotes mental awareness.

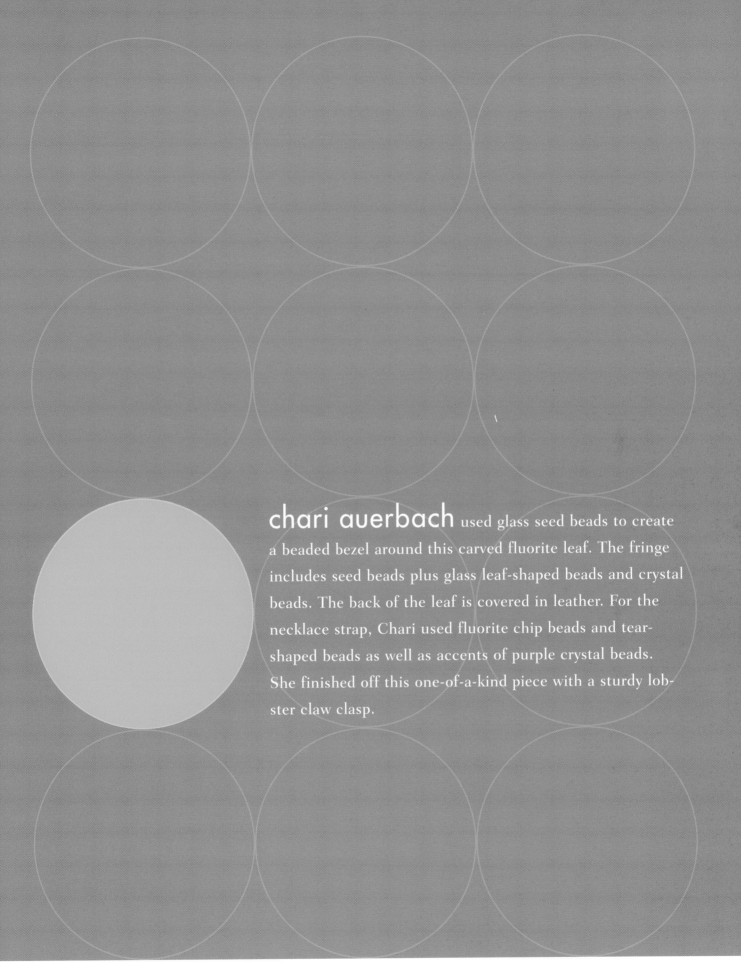

chari auerbach used glass seed beads to create a beaded bezel around this carved fluorite leaf. The fringe includes seed beads plus glass leaf-shaped beads and crystal beads. The back of the leaf is covered in leather. For the necklace strap, Chari used fluorite chip beads and tear-shaped beads as well as accents of purple crystal beads. She finished off this one-of-a-kind piece with a sturdy lobster claw clasp.

rhona farber, from Over the Moon Jewelry, calls this design her "Magical Bauble Bracelet." The bracelet is an eclectic combination of assorted stone, crystal, vintage glass, and pearl beads. The beads are connected together using the *wrap loop* technique, and then the two strands are finished off with a sterling silver heart toggle clasp. While Rhona makes each of these bracelets uniquely different depending on the beads she uses, the piece pictured includes some of the following beads: aqua crystal, pearls, fluorite, iolite, garnet, turquoise, amethyst, citrine, vintage glass, sodalite, amazonite, moonstone, peridot, coral, blue onyx, rose quartz, carnelian, and blue topaz.

chari auerbach

These fringe earrings include tiny 1-mm round tiger's-eye beads and little malachite tube-shaped beads. Each piece of fringe is accented with a citrine-colored and emerald-colored Austrian crystal bead. While this fringe technique is most often used with glass seed beads, Chari was able to locate these unusually small stone beads to create this unique pair of earrings. Each also includes a gold-filled ear hook.

suzanne l. helwig, from Wig Jig, made this antique-style necklace, reminiscent of the jewelry you may find in your grandmother's jewelry box. White 6-mm freshwater pearls are the primary beads used in this rich necklace. The faceted oval and teardrop-shaped teal beads are quartz, and the dark teal beads are faceted pearls. Suzanne used gold-filled wire and a wire jig to create the two components that connect the three strands of beads to a single strap at the top. The accent beads and clasp are also gold-filled.

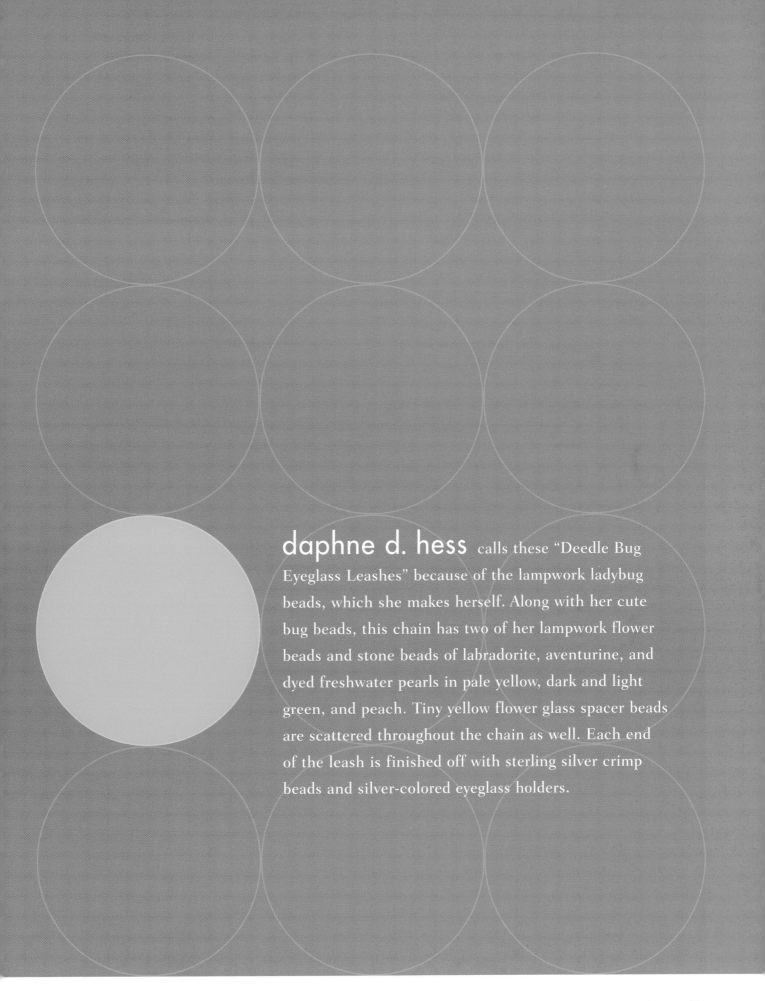

daphne d. hess calls these "Deedle Bug Eyeglass Leashes" because of the lampwork ladybug beads, which she makes herself. Along with her cute bug beads, this chain has two of her lampwork flower beads and stone beads of labradorite, aventurine, and dyed freshwater pearls in pale yellow, dark and light green, and peach. Tiny yellow flower glass spacer beads are scattered throughout the chain as well. Each end of the leash is finished off with sterling silver crimp beads and silver-colored eyeglass holders.

terry l. carter

created her "Fairy Necklace," which is approximately 24" (61 cm) long, using 4-mm carnelian stone beads as the primary beads. Then she accented the carnelian with 8-mm and 6-mm hematite beads, freshwater pearls, 6-mm agate beads, and silver daisy spacer beads. A sterling silver fairy charm floats in the center of the necklace.

gary l. helwig, from Wig Jig, made this pretty gold and amethyst bracelet. The 6-mm amethyst beads are a beautiful dark shade of purple, and each is multifaceted. He connected the beads together using gold-filled chain, wire flower components he created by using a wire jig, and then the *wrap loop* technique. He then finished the bracelet with a gold-colored magnetic clasp.

Michelle used a similar bead-weaving technique in this choker. She used 4-mm freshwater pearls and 4-mm aurora borealis jet crystal beads for a classic combination. This choker also has a bead dangle added to a few inches of sterling chain so that the size of the choker can be adjusted from 13" (33 cm) up to 15" (38 cm) in length.

michelle lambert

combined 4-mm rose quartz beads and rose-colored bi-cone Austrian crystal beads to weave this bracelet. She also included a small stone and crystal dangle next to the sterling silver clasp. While rose quartz makes this bracelet design soft and feminine, the brilliance of the crystals adds sparkle to the finished piece.

tammy powley Geometric-shaped beads of circles, triangles, and rectangles are balanced to create a modern deco-style design in these crystal and turquoise earrings. The purple beads are 6 mm and heavily faceted. The triangular beads are turquoise with spidery black lines, called matrix, running throughout. Rectangular vintage glass beads, which are lined with foil on the back, add a small but powerful sparkle to the bottom of each earring. Hooks, eye pins, and head pins are sterling silver.

Working with Paper

Most of us use paper every day without giving it much thought. The purpose of this chapter is to introduce you to some jewelry making techniques and projects that will open the door to a whole new world of creative opportunities with paper.

Paper is a medium that is accessible to everyone. As you work on the projects in this chapter, you will find that all kinds of paper, from the contents of your recycling bin to expensive wrapping paper, can be transformed into beautiful jewelry. Before you begin working with paper, you should understand the basic nature of paper and cardboard, also known as chipboard. The fibers of each of these materials are formed in such a way that they line up and point in one direction, called the grain. You can use this characteristic to your advantage because the paper and board will bend, fold, and tear more easily if you make your folds and tears parallel to the grain.

Work will always progress more quickly and easily when you are working with the right tools. A ruler is essential for making accurate measurements, and straight lines and cuts. In most cases, a craft knife is the best paper-cutting tool, but sometimes you will need the versatility of scissors. Keep two different sizes of scissors handy. Use small scissors to cut out delicate decoupage pieces and larger, sturdier scissors to cut through heavier materials such as chipboard.

The glue that you use, and the tools that you use to apply it, will also affect how easy it is to complete the project. Polyvinyl acetate (PVA) is a very strong, flexible white glue that is easy to work with and dries quickly. It is available in many art supply stores and bookbinder supply shops. There are two tools you can use for applying glue, depending on the project. Use a squeeze bottle for narrow beads or dots of glue, but to cover larger areas, use a brush to apply the glue.

Lastly, a good pair of needle-nosed pliers is indispensable for holding onto the small jewelry findings that are necessary for turning a beautiful piece of paper craft into a personal accessory.

Jewelry findings are essential to the jewelry making process. Available in craft stores in either silver or gold color, they form, attach, or close jewelry pieces. The findings used to link together paper jewelry in this chapter are jump rings, small metal rings that can be opened to thread through a jewelry piece and then closed again to secure everything in place; and eye pins and head pins, short, straight pieces of wire with a stop at one end to prevent jewelry items such as paper beads from sliding off the end. An eye pin has a small circle of wire at the end so that it can be linked to other items, and the head pin is capped by a flat disk of metal like a sewing pin. Jewelry findings used in this chapter include the barrel clasp in the Flapper's Bead Necklace (page 130) which looks like a cylinder whose two halves screw into one another. The spring ring clasp that closes the Origami Fold Bracelet (page 182) resembles a jump ring with a small latch so that it can be opened and closed by hand. The Golden Braid Choker (page 178) clasp comes in two pieces that hook together with a latch and chain. Each of the two pieces has a decorative metal clamp that is pinched down over each end of the paper that makes up the necklace.

The paper beading, folding, and weaving techniques featured here are very simple and the results can look very professional, but be sure to take your time when laying out the projects to assure a beautiful piece of paper jewelry. Once you have learned a technique, experiment to discover variations in design. Most of all, enjoy the process and the inherent rewards of your creative undertakings.

Pointers

▶ **Keep a sharp point on your pencil to assure accurate measurements.**

▶ **If you cannot find $1/32$" (.75 mm) chipboard, substitute cardboard from cereal boxes.**

▶ **Use an indelible marker when adding details to a project—anything else will smear when you add the finish coat of polyurethane.**

Keep craft knives and scissors very sharp to make the neatest cuts.

▶ **Shorten or lengthen necklace and bracelet patterns to fit your size and proportions. Adjust other patterns to suit your needs.**

Making paper beads is a simple craft that can yield elegant results. Beads can be linked for necklaces and earrings, strung together to make chokers, bracelets, and hair ornaments, or used to decorate papier-mâché or woven paper jewelry.

Paper beads traditionally were created by winding a paper strip around a knitting needle or a nail. The length of a bead is determined by the measurement of the widest part of the paper strip, and the thickness by the length of the strip, the weight of the paper stock, and the size of the center hole.

A cotter pin can be substituted for the knitting needle or nail. The pin has two legs that act as a gripping device and make it easier to wind the bead with the appropriate tension. The gauge or thickness of the cotter pin will also determine the size of the bead's center hole. Hardware stores carry a wide assortment of cotter pins.

Paper Bead Jewelry

The paper you choose for your jewelry depends on the project and your taste. Marbled papers lend themselves beautifully to paper beads; so do paste paper, vellum, handmade paper, and wrapping paper. Even papers with rather mundane patterns can yield surprising results when wrapped into beads. Once you have made and decorated the beads, they can simply be strung together. You will need about thirty, $3/4$" (2 cm) beads to make a medium-length necklace, and ten or twelve for a single-strand bracelet.

To begin the design process, collect an assortment of papers that vary in pattern, color, and texture, and lay them out in front of you. Shuffle and reshuffle the papers until you find some pieces that work well together, then cut the paper into strips about 5" to 7" (13 cm to 18 cm) long. The shape of the paper strip will determine the shape of the bead: triangular pieces of paper make rounded beads; an isosceles triangle (two sides of equal length) makes an oval or spherical bead; an asymmetrical triangle makes a teardrop; a rectangular strip makes a cylindrical bead.

How to Make Paper Beads

Cut out paper strips with pinking shears or curved- and wavy-edge novelty scissors (available at most arts and crafts stores) to give beads an interesting texture.

To make patterned beads, back a straight-edged strip with a strip of the same size cut with a pair of novelty scissors.

Glue together two or more strips of different colors—make one strip slightly larger than the other—for a beautiful, multicolored spiral effect.

1 To start, slip one end of the paper strip (the widest end of the triangular pieces) under one leg of the cotter pin.

▶ To make beads with large center holes, try using a toothpick or a knitting needle instead of a cotter pin.

▶ If a bead is wound too tightly to remove from the cotter pin, gently twist the entire bead in the opposite direction from which it was wound. This should slightly unwind the bead and loosen it enough to slide from the pin.

2 Wind the paper around the cotter pin firmly, keeping an even tension on the strip. If the bead is wound too tightly, you may find that you cannot remove it from the pin. Keep winding until you reach the end of the paper strip.

▶ You may find thick papers difficult to roll up. The thinner the paper, the easier it is to handle. If you want a thicker paper bead, use a longer paper strip.

▶ To finish paper beads, use water-based polyurethane: it won't yellow and it dries within a few hours. A coat of polyvinyl acetate (PVA) glue is a good alternative to polyurethane but is not as durable.

3 Secure the end of the strip to the finished bead with a small dot of glue. Hold the end in place until the glue sets, then gently slide the bead off the cotter pin. Let dry for about an hour. When they are dry, slip two beads at a time back onto the cotter pin and use a small brush to apply PVA glue or polyurethane.

▶ You may want to leave beads uncoated, but be aware that any bead that touches the body is likely to discolor and pill as it absorbs oils from the skin.

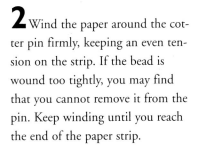

Making the Jewelry

I learned about paper beads from my grandmother, who made them as a girl. After a long day of work, she and her sisters would gather in the kitchen to design and string beautiful paper bead curtains that would afford them a little privacy in their small living quarters. For them, it was both a social and creative gathering. They used remnants of wallpaper, cut into strips and rolled around a nail. A dot of white glue secured the bead, and several coats of varnish were applied as a finish before the beads were strung together. In this manner, they created colorful draperies one bead at a time.

Use nylon, silk, or cotton thread and a beading needle—or try stringing beads on silk cord, narrow ribbon, or fine-gauge wire. String multiple strands and twist them into a colorful rope, or make strands of tiny paper beads and braid them together for a woven effect. Add knots, spacer beads, or charms between paper beads for color or texture contrast.

The light weight of paper beads can make them hard to balance: if they are strung too tightly, the strand will buckle instead of hanging straight down; if they are strung too loosely, portions of the strand will show between beads or gravity will pull all the beads down toward the center. The gaps will be exposed on the strand behind the neck.

Also, if the center hole is not large enough for the strand and you push too hard, the bead will "telescope" out.

Beading Tips

For a *fancier* design, thread several strands through a single large bead, then separate them to work each strand individually, before bringing them back together through another single bead.

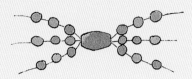

Bead *multiple* strands individually, bring together through a large bead, and separate again on the other side.

Join *beads* with eye pins or head pins for a glint of gold or silver between each bead.

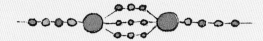

Curl *short* strands of beads in a spiral and glue to a pin or earring back.

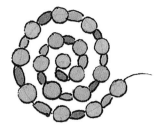

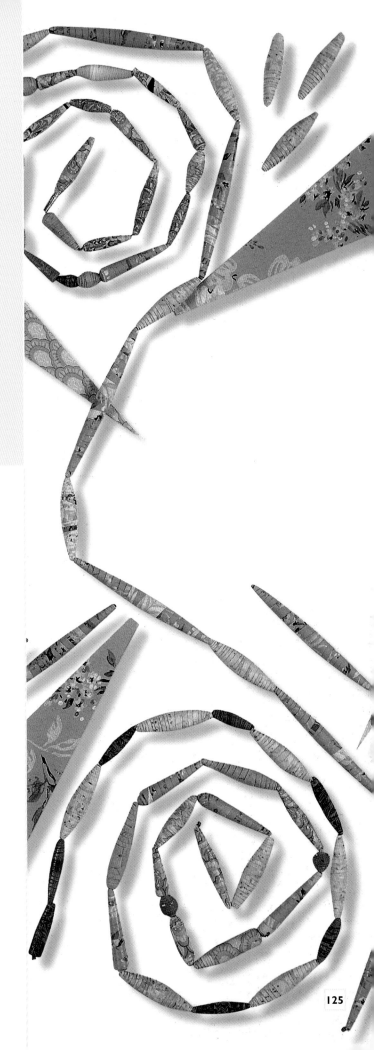

Triple Strand
Bracelet

Sometimes there are treasures hiding in the back corner of a storage drawer, like this wonderful red paper threaded with delicate gold fibers. The fibrous texture of the paper has so much character that it is a shame to bury it under a thick polyurethane finish, as would usually be done for a bracelet. Instead, lightly coat the beads with a thin application of PVA glue, then string them on gold embroidery ribbon. The result is a colorful bracelet that is quite sophisticated and remarkably simple to make.

Materials

$3/32" \times 2"$ (2.5 mm × 5 cm) cotter pin

Scissors

Needle-nosed pliers

Ruler

Pencil

Embroidery needle

6 yards (5.5 meters) of $1/8"$ (.3 cm)
  embroidery ribbon

Piece of gold threaded red paper,
  $10" \times 7"$ (25 cm × 18 cm)

Spring ring clasp

Pair of 6 mm jump rings

Sewing needle

Cotton thread to match ribbon

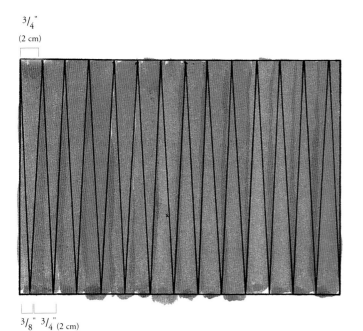

$3/4"$

(2 cm)

$3/8"$ $3/4"$ (2 cm)

(1 cm)

Getting Started

Turn the paper you have chosen to the "wrong" side
(the side that will become the inside of the rolled-up
bead) and make a pencil mark every $3/4"$ (2 cm) down
the 10" (25 cm) edge. On the opposite edge, make
one mark $3/8"$ (1 cm) from the edge of the paper, then
make marks every $3/4"$ (2 cm) for the length of the
sheet. Use a ruler to connect the marked points in a
zigzag fashion, then cut the paper into the resulting
triangular strips. Discard the first and last pieces.

1 Wind twenty-four beads, following the instructions in How to Make Paper Beads on page 123. Use a drop of PVA glue to coat the beads and let them dry thoroughly.

2 Cut the embroidery ribbon into six 1-yard (.9 meter) lengths and thread all six through the ring clasp, as shown. Center the clasp in the middle of the ribbon and knot the strands, pulling tight against the jump ring.

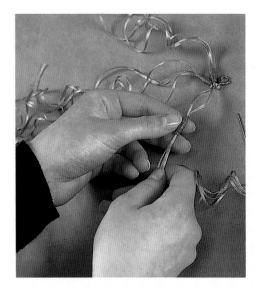

3 Separate the embroidery ribbon into three groups of four strands each. With an embroidery needle, thread a bead onto each set of ribbons and bring it all the way to the end of the strand.

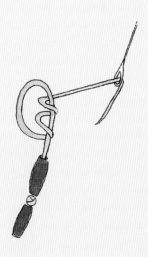

4 Tie a knot after each bead by pulling the tail of the ribbon through the loop of the knot twice, as shown in the illustration. Push the knot firmly against the bead. Repeat steps 3 and 4 until you have strung and knotted eight beads onto each group of ribbons. Keep the ribbon tension taut, but not so tight that the beads buckle, and try to make knots that are the same size.

5 Thread all the ribbons through the middle of the jump ring. Then, working one bead strand at a time, use the embroidery needle to thread all four ribbons in each group back down through their corresponding knot and final bead. This secures the end of the ribbon.

6 With the sewing needle and thread, make two or three small stitches in the ribbon just below the final knot of each strand. This will further secure the back-tracking of the ribbons. Cut the remaining ribbon ends as close to the bead as you can.

7 With the needle-nosed pliers, open the second jump ring slightly and link it with the first, using the pliers to close it again.

Variation
on a Theme

For this version of the project, $\frac{1}{2}$"(1 cm) beads were used in two colors and three different colored threads, instead of the three gold strands. The result is a beautiful collage of green and blue hues for a very attractive bracelet.

Flapper's Bead
Necklace

You will find this necklace effortless to assemble because embroidery floss is made of six individual threads that can be easily separated from one another. These threads are separated and then recombined in this piece to form the multiple strands. When you reach the point in the step-by-step instructions where the floss is threaded in three directions, you will separate the floss into three pairs of threads. When the instructions call for one strand again, you will thread all three pairs back through the needle.

Materials

2 pieces of Thai marbled paper, 6" × 24" (15 cm × 61 cm)

2 pieces of gold spotted maroon paper,
  6" × 6 3/4" (15 cm × 17 cm) and
  6" × 6" (15 cm × 15 cm)

3/32" × 2" (2.5 mm × 5 cm) cotter pin

PVA glue

Water-based polyurethane

Small paintbrush

Gold barrel necklace clasp

2 pieces of 36" (91 cm) long black
  embroidery floss

Ruler

Scissors

Embroidery needle

Pencil

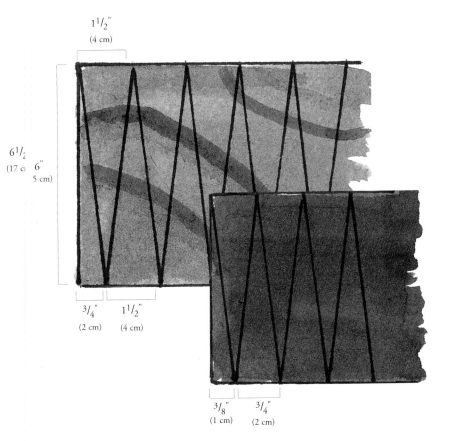

Getting Started

Review the section on How to Make Paper Beads on page 123. To make twenty-four *cylindrical* beads, start by cutting the 6" × 6 ¾" (15 cm × 17 cm) piece of maroon paper into twenty-four strips measuring ¼" × 6" (.5 cm × 15 cm). Follow the illustrations to make sixty-two Thai marbled paper *oval* beads and thirty-two maroon oval beads, letting each coat dry before adding the next.

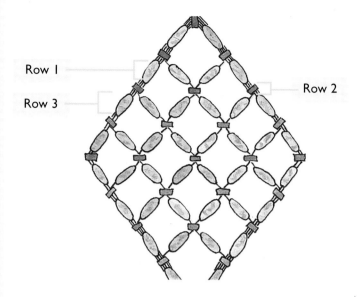

Row 1

Row 2

Row 3

1 Use the scissors to cut five, 3 foot (90 cm) pieces of wire, then thread all five pieces through one green bead. On both sides of the green bead, thread a gold and then a pink bead. Center this series of beads on the wires, then bend the wires in half at the green bead.

2 Beginning at row 1, follow the illustration to thread all the beads. It helps to hook your work over a nail to provide adequate tension. The first four wires of the left-hand packet are threaded through one gold bead, as is the remaining wire. From the right-hand packet of wires, one wire is threaded through one gold bead, and the next four wires are then threaded through a single gold bead.

3 Thread one set of five wires through one green bead. Thread the remaining five wires through the same green bead but in the opposite direction.

4 Pull all the wires around to the back side of the piece and twist them together once or twice. Work the first set of five wires back through one of the last gold beads. Repeat with the other five wires through the gold bead on the other side of the final green bead.

5 Use the scissors to trim the excess wire off as close as possible to the beads. You may find it helpful to bend the hair piece back so that you may cut the wires very close to the gold beads. Having done that, gently shape the piece into its proper diamond shape with a gentle convex curve.

6 Use the hand saw to cut a 6 ½" (17 cm) piece of the dowel, then sharpen each end of the dowel in the pencil sharpener until the point resembles the end of a chopstick.

Variation **on a Theme**

You can use the same basic techniques to make any number of shapes for other hair slides. In this hair piece, the beads are worked into a figure-eight pattern that requires only four wires instead of five. Wire is knotted between each bead just as the thread was in the Triple Strand Bracelet on page 126.

It may be hard to believe, but the simple papier-mâché skills learned by children in grade school or at summer camp can be put to use creating elegant jewelry. Paper strips and wallpaper paste, both readily available and inexpensive materials, can be used to make a variety of professional-looking bracelets, necklaces, and pins.

The easiest papier-mâché method, strip papier-mâché, has only a few components when working on such small pieces as jewelry. Before beginning, make some sort of internal structure or skeleton for the project out of cardboard and/or wire; anything that creates the general outline of the finished product can be used. Once the skeleton is ready, layer it with strips of paper that have been dipped in thick liquid paste such as liquid starch or water-thinned white glue. The easiest glue to obtain and work with is wallpaper paste. It is sold in most hardware or paint and paper stores as a powder to which you add water to form the paste.

Papier-Mâché Jewelry

Just about any paper can be used to layer over your base shape. Newspaper ripped into strips is the traditional choice, but any lightweight paper will work. Be careful of papers that are too thin—they will rip apart when soaked with the paste. On the other hand, very thick papers do not have the flexibility to wrap neatly around the skeleton of a piece. The choice depends on the finished look you are trying to achieve. The Celestial Bangle on page 150 uses the properties of lightweight tissue paper to create the texture on the surface of the pieces. A very large, flat, and chunky project, however, could benefit from robust, heavier papers.

The size of your project determines the size of the paper strips that you will need. Use short, narrow strips to cover the skeletons of jewelry shapes. Avoid having the paper fold over itself, adding unnecessary bulk to the piece. Choose the appropriate thickness of paper and tear it into the proper size strip to assure quick progress and a neat end result.

Another papier-mâché method, pulp papier-mâché, is quickly gaining in popularity, and many arts and crafts stores carry the mix. Paper is ground up and mixed with paste so that it has the consistency of clay. The pulp can be freely modeled into any shape or applied to a skeleton and dries very hard. Once dry, you can smooth the dappled surface by leveling it with spackle. Keep in mind that either form of papier-mâché can get messy, so protect your work surface by covering it with tin foil or wax paper, which won't stick to your project.

How to Make Strip Papier-Mâché

Ingredients

$\frac{1}{3}$ cup flour
2 cups cold water
Saucepan
Spoon

Materials

Wallpaper paste mixed as directed on its package

Paper torn into strips

Skeleton for your project

1 Mix the flour and the water together in the pan and let it sit until there are no lumps, about twenty minutes.

2 Place the pan over medium-high heat and bring to a boil, stirring constantly.

3 Remove the pan from the heat and let the paste cool before using.

1 Dip a strip of paper into the paste and then slide it through your fingers to remove the excess.

Recipe for Pulp Papier-Mâché

Ingredients

Pulp papier-mâché mixed as directed on its package
Skeleton for the project
Spackle
Putty knife
Fine sandpaper

2 Lay the strip over the skeleton, neatly wrapping it around bends and angles. Dip another strip and lay it next to, but slightly overlapping, the first. Continue laying down strips in the same direction. Let each layer dry thoroughly before adding the next.

1 This one is easy! Working with small amounts at a time, simply mold the pulp around the skeleton, filling in the basic shape. Cover the skeleton completely. For small projects, an internal structure may not be necessary; just model the pulp freely, like clay, to form the general figure.

2 With more pulp, add the details (features, curves) of the piece. Set it aside until completely dry. Drying time varies greatly depending on the thickness of the piece.

3 Lay down the next layer of papier-mâché with the strips perpendicular to the first layer to strengthen the piece's structure. For example, if the first layer of papier-mâché traveled from left to right, the next layer will travel from top to bottom.

3 For a very smooth finish, cover the surface with a thin, no more than $\frac{1}{8}$" (.3 cm), layer of spackle and drag the knife over it while it is still wet, removing the excess. Don't leave any ruts or ridges. The spackle that is left behind fills in the low spots of the pulp surface. Once the spackle is dry (about an hour), you can further smooth the surface by lightly sanding it.

4 Keep adding layers of papier-mâché until the paper skin is the appropriate thickness. Remember to let each layer dry thoroughly before adding the next, alternating the direction of the strips for each layer.

139

Like many people, I first encountered papier-mâché as a child. I remember being enthralled by the cool, thick paste I could squish between my fingers and the outlandish characters I could create so easily. My first project, a clown piñata for my seventh birthday party, was more funny looking than funny, but it introduced me to a technique that I used for other childhood projects, from an elephant head for Halloween to a volcano for science class.

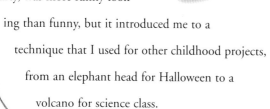

Making the Jewelry

Once you have built the skeleton and skin of a project, use the last layer of strip papier-mâché or the wet papier-mâché pulp to achieve a vast number of looks and finishes. In strip papier-mâché, try using a different thickness of paper for the last layer. Fold or bunch the strips as you lay them down to add texture to the piece. Use colored paper for the final layer to eliminate the need to paint. For pulp papier-mâché, add dye to the pulp mixture. In addition, after modeling the pulp, try pressing flowers, buttons, or other found objects into the wet surface. The flower can either become part of the surface design or you can remove it to leave behind an impression of its petals and stamens.

Papier-Mâché Tips

Store unused *papier-mâché* in the refrigerator to extend its useful life.

Use *cookie cutters* as forms for pulp papier-mâché to make easy ornaments, charms, or pins.

Try using *materials* other than paper, such as fabrics or leaves, for the final layer of strip papier-mâché.

Cover your work *surface* with either tin foil or wax paper to keep your project from sticking to anything.

To make *unusual* and funky beads, form pulp papier-mâché into small shapes and push a needle through them while the pulp is still wet. Allow these to dry and then decorate as you desire with paints, glitter, or inks.

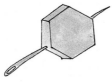

Before adding your *last layer* of papier-mâché, glue items such as spirals of string or cardboard cutouts to the surface to create texture and features in the finished surface.

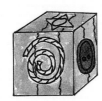

Kite

Pendant

The tails of this kite are wire, which can be bent to mimic wind blowing through them. The tissue papers are so thin that their colors become somewhat translucent when they are papier-mâchéd in place, resulting in a beautiful blending of color in the finished piece.

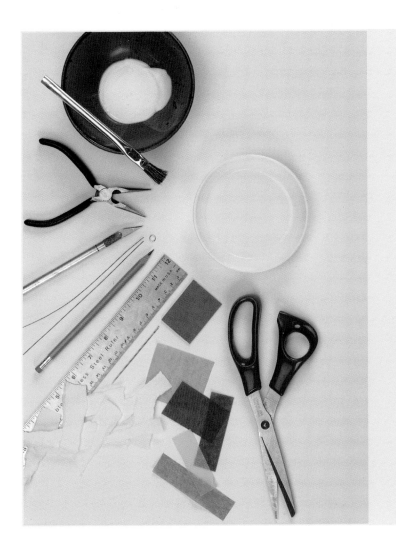

Materials

$\frac{1}{16}$" (1.5 mm) chipboard or cardboard
measuring $1\frac{1}{2}$" × 2" (4 cm × 5 cm)

Sheet of white typing paper, cut into strips
measuring $\frac{1}{2}$" × 7" (1 cm × 18 cm)

$7\frac{1}{2}$" (19 cm) of 26-gauge wire

Tissue paper: dark green, light green, pink,
yellow, and blue

Wallpaper paste mixed as directed on its package

PVA glue

Glue brush

Embroidery needle

4 mm silver jump ring

Ruler

Pencil

Craft knife

Scissors

Needle-nosed pliers

Getting Started

With the ruler and the pencil, mark the midpoints of
each side of the rectangle of chipboard and draw lines
to connect them, forming a diamond. Use the craft
knife to cut out the diamond.

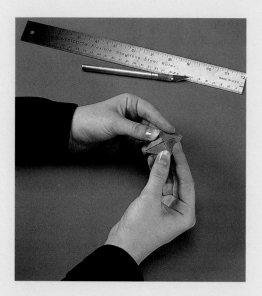

1 Line up the ruler to connect two opposite points of the diamond. Use the craft knife to score the front of the board, making sure to cut only halfway through its thickness. Repeat this between the other two points and bend the chipboard diamond back along both score lines so that a peak is formed in the middle of the diamond. This peaked side will be the front of the kite.

2 To make the tails of the kite, take a strip of white paper and spread a thin coat of glue over one side. Place the wire, lengthwise, in the center of the strip and fold the paper in half, enclosing the wire. This white paper will serve as a base for the very thin tissue paper.

3 Cut the paper-covered wire into three lengths: 3" (8 cm), 2½" (6 cm), and 2" (5 cm). Coat the 3" (8 cm) paper-covered wire with the wallpaper paste and cover it with the blue tissue paper. Do the same with the 2½" (6 cm) wire and the pink paper, and the 2" (5 cm) wire and the yellow paper. Set these aside to dry.

4 Use the scissors to trim the tails so that they are ⅛" (.3 cm) wide. Glue them to the back side of the bottom point of the kite. Be sure that you are using the pieces with the wire inside them.

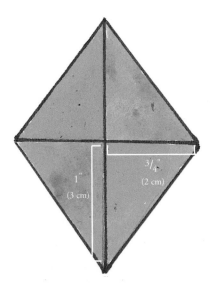

5 With the remaining white paper strips, cover the chipboard with two layers of papier-mâché. Remember to let the first layer of papier-mâché dry before adding the second and that the second layer should be laid down perpendicular to the first. Use the light green tissue paper as a final third layer of papier-mâché.

6 Cut out two triangles of dark green tissue paper according to the dimensions in the illustration and papier-mâché them in place as shown.

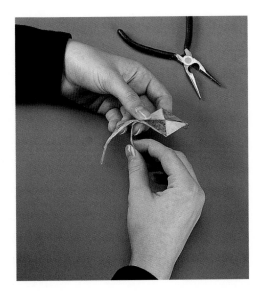

7 With the needle, punch a hole in the top point of the kite. Use the needle-nosed pliers to thread the jump ring through the hole. Bend the tails into shape so that they look as though the wind is blowing through them.

Variation on a Theme

This leaf pendant uses a wire armature like the kite tails to give it its shape. To form the features of the leaf, use the pulp papier-mâché instead of the strip papier-mâché method.

Fishy
Pulp Pins

These charming pins could not be any easier to make! Pulp papier-mâché allows this project
to progress quickly and provides you with an end result that will endure time, wear, and the
elements (even water). You can use bright colors to decorate the fish for your lapel or bag, or, if
you prefer a more subdued finish, try painting in tones of blue and green. Either way, these
aquatic creatures are simple projects that can be used as beautiful jewelry.

Materials

PVA glue

Spackle

Putty knife

Black, white, red, yellow, and green latex paint

Paintbrush

Wax paper

Pulp papier-mâché

Sandpaper

Two 1" (3 cm) pin backs

Water-based polyurethane

Indelible black marker

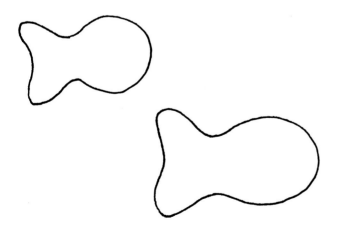

Getting Started

Transfer the fish patterns to the wax paper using the carbon paper method described in How to Transfer Images and Patterns, page 157.

1 Place a small amount of pulp into the outline of one fish and flatten it until it is about ¼" (.5 cm) thick, keeping the pulp within the lines. Continue adding pulp until the entire silhouette is filled in. Repeat with the other fish.

2 Add a little more pulp to the head and tail of one fish so that it is slightly mounded. Gently mold the pulp to define the shape of the fish, smoothing out any rough spots in the surface of the pulp. Repeat with the other fish and set the two aside overnight or until they are thoroughly dry.

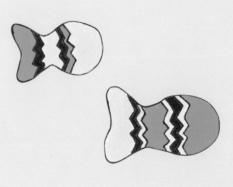

3 To create a very smooth finish, spackle and sand the fish using the technique described in step 3 of the Recipe for Pulp Papier-Mâché on page 139.

4 Following the pattern, paint the background colors of each fish and set them aside to dry for about an hour.

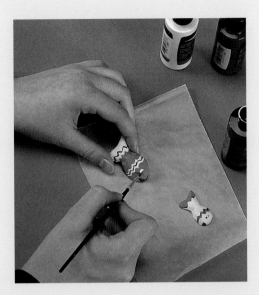

5 Using the red, black, and white paint, add the mouth and eyes. When the paint is dry (approximately one hour), use the indelible marker to add the outlines. Apply three coats of polyurethane to the front and back of each fish, letting each coat dry before adding the next.

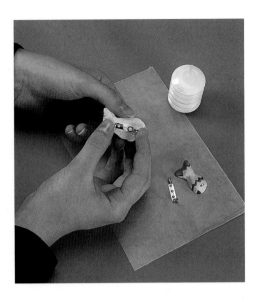

6 Once the polyurethane is dry, run a bead of glue onto one 1" (3 cm) pin back and press it firmly onto the back of one fish. Repeat with the other.

Variation
on a Theme

Molding pulp papier-mâché is so easy that any number of characters can quickly and easily come to life. This emerald toad is fashioned just like the fish.

Celestial Bangle

Bracelet

The magical realm of the night sky is captured in this lighthearted bangle bracelet. The real wonder, though, is how easy it is to use papier-mâché to create it. The skeleton is made of chipboard squares, covered by strip papier-mâché. Tissue paper, wrinkled to add texture and character to the finished piece, is used as the last papier-mâché layer. When the gold ink is added, you will find that the wrinkles on the tissue paper will add to the weathered look of the final bracelet.

Materials

Pencil

Needle-nosed pliers

Piece of $\frac{1}{16}$" (1.5 mm) chipboard or
cardboard, 4" × 4" (10 cm × 10 cm)

Ruler

Craft knife

Wallpaper paste mixed as directed on its package

White paper strips, $\frac{1}{2}$" × 2" (1 cm × 5 cm)

Sturdy scissors

PVA glue

Glue brush

Tissue paper strips, 1" × $1\frac{1}{2}$" (3 cm × 4 cm)

Small paintbrush

Purple latex paint

Gold pen

Embroidery needle

Water-based polyurethane

18 gold 7 mm jump rings

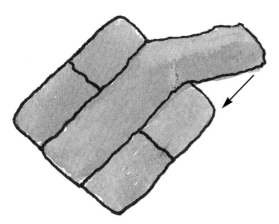

Lay down the second layer perpendicular to the first.

Getting Started

With the ruler and craft knife, cut eight 1" (3 cm) squares from the chipboard. Cover the squares with two layers of papier-mâché each made from the white paper, following the basic directions given in How to Make Strip Papier-Mâché on page 139. Remember to lay down the second layer of papier-mâché perpendicular to the first.

1 On the remaining piece of chipboard, draw an assortment of four stars and four moons, making sure that their dimensions do not exceed ³⁄₄" (2 cm) in any direction. You may find it useful to draw a grid on the board first so that you can draw the stars and moon within them. Use the scissors to cut them out, then glue one to the center of each square made in Getting Started.

2 Dip a strip of tissue paper into the papier-mâché paste and wrap it around a square. Allow it to wrinkle and fold over itself to give the piece some texture. Make sure, though, that the shape (star or moon) is still well defined. Continue adding tissue paper strips in a single layer until the entire square is covered. Repeat this process with the remaining seven squares.

3 After a few hours, when the papier-mâché is thoroughly dry, apply a thin coat of purple paint to one side of each of the squares. When this is dry, in about thirty minutes, paint the other side of the squares with the same color.

4 When the paint is dry, use the gold pen to outline the squares and to color in the shapes themselves. For a weathered look, partially color in the shapes and use your finger to spread the wet ink. To finish the square, apply two coats of polyurethane with a small brush, allowing the first to dry at least an hour before adding the second.

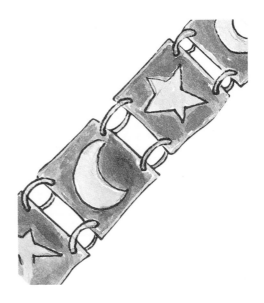

5 Use the needle to punch holes in all the squares as shown. When all eight pieces have been punched, you are ready to form the bracelet.

6 Line up the squares in front of you, alternating moons and stars. Use the needle-nosed pliers to open the jump rings to connect each square to the next as shown.

7 When all the pieces have been attached to each other, gently curve the bracelet into a circle and use the last two jump rings to secure the first square to the last.

Variation
on a Theme

Bangles look great no matter what shape their pieces are, but simply changing the location of where the pieces join can dramatically alter the look of the piece. For this red version of the bracelet, squares are joined at their corner points instead of along their edges.

$\mathcal{D}$ecoupage, the use of paper cutouts to cover a surface, began in eighteenth-century France, when court ladies tried to mimic popular Japanese and Chinese lacquered furniture of the era. The technique is still popular today because it is easy, and the results can be elegant. Decoupage jewelry is a beautiful way to display tiny pictures that would otherwise be too small to appreciate. A single cut image, such as a rose or a bird, can become an eye-catching pin or barrette. More intricate collages make both meaningful and beautiful pins or lockets.

There are only a few basics needed for a decoupage project. Choose a surface to decorate, then decide which images to cover it. Magazines, newspapers, and catalogs are good sources; even old books and photographs can be used. If cutting up treasured photos is unthinkable, modern photocopying techniques can give you a quality reproduction.

Decoupage Jewelry

Collecting and cutting out the pictures you want to use for jewelry is the most time-consuming aspect of the decoupage process, but the selection and arrangement of these cutouts will determine the success of the project. When you are choosing images, make sure their size is appropriate to the decorating surface. Large cutouts will feel heavy and may even seem to disappear as they wrap around the edges of a small piece. Small cutouts may be hard to appreciate, especially on large pieces. Play with the images to see how they best fit together. Once you have found an arrangement that suits your project, use a pencil to lightly outline where each piece goes on the background. This will make it easier to position the piece after you have brushed the glue on the back of it. When all the elements have been affixed to the background, several coats of lacquer are applied to create a polished, smooth surface.

How to Decoupage

Decoupage is fun and easy and can be tailored to suit anyone's interests, so choose a theme that appeals to you or the recipient of the piece you are making.

Materials

Assorted images

Scissors or craft knife

PVA glue

Tweezers

Glue brush

Water-based polyurethane or acrylic medium

Paintbrush

1 Begin by gathering an assortment of images that go well together. Once you have selected the pictures, carefully cut them out with either the scissors or the craft knife, following the outlines of the pictures exactly. Try to angle your cuts away from the image so that the top surface of the picture does not show the cut edge.

2 Lay out the pieces on the decorating surface and move them around, until you find an arrangement that appeals to you. Glue the background pictures first. Brush a thin coat of glue on the back of each and use the tweezers to lay them in place. Repeat this with each picture, beginning with background images and working toward those in the foreground. Set the entire piece aside to dry.

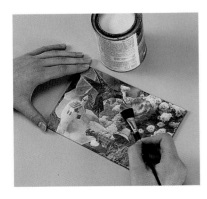

3 Brush multiple coats of polyurethane or acrylic medium over the decoupage, allowing each layer to dry for about an hour and a half before adding the next. Your goal is a smooth surface. Acrylic medium requires fewer coats than polyurethane, but both add a perfect finish. The number of coats required depends on the thickness of the cutout paper and the number of overlapping images involved. You may need five to twenty coats of finish.

How to Make Acrylic Transfers

Materials

Acrylic medium

Brush

Picture to be transferred

Flat, shallow pan of water

Wax paper

1 Place the picture on the wax paper, face up, and brush a coat of acrylic medium over it. Make sure that the medium extends all the way to the edges and that your brush strokes are all in the same direction. Set this aside to dry for one hour.

2 Brush a second coat of acrylic medium over the picture with the strokes moving perpendicular to those of the first coat. Set this aside to dry.

3 Repeat steps 1 and 2 until you have at least ten coats of acrylic medium over the picture.

4 Once the last coat of acrylic medium is dry (about one hour), place the whole piece in a pan of water and let it soak long enough that the paper absorbs some water and starts to soften. Depending on the paper, you may need to let it sit between fifteen and forty-five minutes.

5 With the piece face down in the water, start rubbing away the paper from the back with your fingers. Keep on rubbing, gently so as not to tear the film, until all the paper has been removed. Take the acrylic film out of the water, set aside to dry for a half an hour, and then use as desired for your project.

$\mathcal{D}$ecoupage is a simple technique, but it can be used to make ingenious necklaces, bracelets, earrings, and pins. Instead of using pictures that are picked out from a magazine, try cutting various colored papers into an assortment of shapes to assemble into a new, original image of your own. The Lady Pin is an example of how ordinary scraps of paper can be cut and formed into a beautiful piece. The cuff bracelet in this chapter uses a process of transferring images on paper to acrylic film, which is then cut to fit the decoupage. This film is created by brushing multiple layers of acrylic medium over the picture and soaking the piece in water so that the paper can be rubbed off. What remains is a film that holds only the colors of the original. The film can be stretched or otherwise manipulated and is so thin that its edges are difficult to detect beneath the finish coats of the project. Thanks to modern technology, treasured photo- graphs can be used in decoupage jewelry without damaging the original photo by making high-quality photocopies. The Floral Decoupage Locket uses a quick and easy transfer technique to create a silhouette from a photo. Once images are reproduced on white paper, they can be manipulated much more easily.

Making the Jewelry

Decoupage Tips

Photocopy your *favorite* photos to cut out images for decoupage.

To create a *crackle glaze* finish on your decoupage, brush thick layers of finish over the piece and apply the next before the previous has dried completely.

How to Transfer Images and Patterns

Materials

Pattern

Fine point black indelible marker

Tracing paper

Carbon paper

Paper that the image is being transferred to

1 Choose an image or a pattern with clear, discernible edges, such as people, florals, animals, or furniture.

2 Place the tracing paper over the image and, with the marker, trace the pattern.

3 Lay the paper that the image is being transferred to face down in front of you. Place the carbon paper, ink side down, on top of that, and then the tracing, face down, on top of that.

4 Use the marker to retrace the pattern on the back side of the tracing paper, pushing down firmly so that the carbon paper is sure to leave its mark.

5 When you remove the tracing and carbon papers, you will see that the reverse of the original pattern is on the back side of your final paper. Once this is cut out, when you view the piece from the front side, you will have an exact replica of the pattern without any tracing lines showing.

Add years to *the look* of your jewelry by using an oil-based polyurethane instead of a water-based one. The oil will add a yellowed tinge to the colors.

Lightly *sand* down the back of images on very thick paper. This will make them easier to work with in the decoupage.

Use *tweezers* to hold and place small pieces more easily.

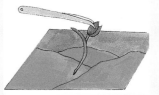

Carbon *paper* can be easily found in department stores and office supply stores.

Golden Ivy *Earrings*

These golden botanicals put a twist on the traditional decoupage technique; the paper cutouts of ivy leaves are mounted on wire so that they decorate space instead of a surface. The wire allows the leaves to be individually placed in their setting, and the gold gilt adds a touch of elegance to an earthy subject. This project can inspire a multitude of variations; you need look only as far as the garden to see what other climbing or draping plants would easily lend their likeness to this form.

Materials

Cutouts of 8 gold ivy leaves

26" (66 cm) of 26-gauge wire

Floral tape

Scissors

Gold paint

Paintbrush

Earring hooks

1" (3 cm) wide masking tape

2 gold 4 mm jump rings

Water-based polyurethane

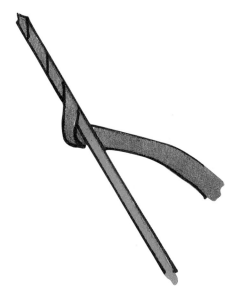

Getting Started

To create the stems, cut the wire into eight 3" (8 cm) lengths and wrap each piece with the floral tape, a stretchy green tape used by florists for wrapping wired stems and readily available at craft supply stores.

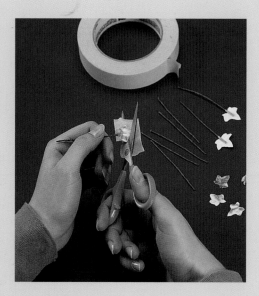

1 Use the masking tape to secure a piece of covered wire to the back of a leaf, making sure that the tape completely covers the back of the leaf. Turn the piece to the front side and use the scissors to trim off the overhanging tape. Repeat with the other seven leaves.

2 Paint the back side of each leaf and its stem with the gold paint. When the paint is dry, brush a coat of polyurethane over the front, back, and stem of each piece. Set these aside to dry.

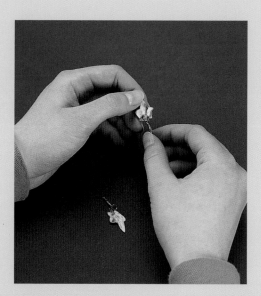

3 For one earring, cut the stems of four leaves down to 1 ¼" (4 cm), 1" (3 cm), ¾" (2 cm), and ¼" (1 cm). Set aside the leaf with the shortest stem and stack the other three on top of each other, lining up the stem ends. Each leaf should be staggered. Twist the ends of the stems together to secure. Repeat this step for the other earring.

4 From the remaining unwrapped wire, cut a piece 1" (3 cm) long and insert it through one jump ring. Bend the wire in half, enclosing the jump ring. Place this piece on top of one remaining short-stemmed leaf, lining up the base of the leaf with the base of the jump ring. Twist the wires and the stem together. Repeat this process with the other jump ring and short-stemmed leaf.

5 As shown in the photo, place the jump ring and short-stemmed leaf on top of a stack of three leaves, with the short-stemmed leaf face down and the wires pointing downward, toward the leaves of the larger stack. Secure these pieces in place by wrapping the stack with a band of the floral tape. Repeat with the other set of leaves and wired jump ring for the other earring.

6 Use the paint to turn the green bands of floral tape holding together all the leaves into gold. When the paint is dry (about one hour), bend the top leaf of each earring forward to reveal its front side and hide the point where all the stems are held together. Gently bend the stems of each leaf forward and to one side or the other to make a natural looking ivy formation. Repeat with the other earring.

7 With the needle-nosed pliers, open the jump ring of one earring and slip it through one ear hook before closing the ring again. Repeat with the other earring.

Variation on a Theme

This delicate cluster of garlic flowers uses the same decoupage technique as the Golden Ivy Earrings on page 158. The flexible wire stems can be molded into a variety of shapes.

Lady
Pin

It can be difficult to throw away those special scraps left over from other projects. Out of desperation to find use for these valued small pieces, I designed a whole line of whimsical pins including everything from flying pigs to French clowns. The young woman featured in this project turned out to be one of the most popular characters and is both easy and fun to make. The only difference between this and traditional decoupage is that you will be cutting out a pattern as opposed to a preexisting image. The application techniques involved are the same.

Materials

Piece of $\frac{1}{32}$" (.75 mm) chipboard or cardboard, 2" × 3" (5 cm × 8 cm)

Blue marbled paper for the suit

Brown marbled paper for the face and hands

Navy marbled paper for the shoes

Purple marbled paper for the belt

Black paper for the back of the pin

Craft knife

PVA glue

Glue brush

Water-based polyurethane

Black fine point indelible marker

Metallic gold marker

Small brush for polyurethane

Tweezers (optional)

1" (3 cm) pin back

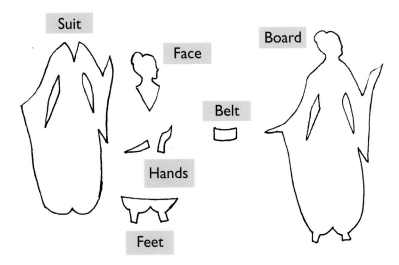

Getting Started

Use a photocopier to enlarge this pattern to fit on
your piece of cardboard. Transfer the patterns to
the papers as listed in Materials, and to the board,
using the method described in How to Transfer
Images and Patterns on page 157. Cut out all the
pieces with the craft knife.

1 Attach the paper pieces of the lady's face to the cardboard backing by brushing a thin coat of glue on the back of the paper piece and press it into place on the front side of the cardboard. Glue each of the pattern pieces continuing in the following order: hands, feet, suit, and belt. Use the tweezers to hold onto and place small pieces.

2 Once all the pieces are glued in place, trim away any paper that overhangs the backing by flipping over the figure and running the knife blade along the edge of the cardboard.

3 Brush a thin coat of glue on the back of the figure and press it down firmly onto the back of the black paper. Trace around the edges of the woman with the knife to trim off any excess paper.

4 Use the marker to outline all the pieces that make up the figure, adding such detail as the facial features and clothing definition. The pattern shows the basics, but feel free to further embellish your pin as your creativity dictates. With the marker, blacken the edge all the way around the pin.

5 Apply three coats of polyurethane to the pin, making sure that the edges and back are coated as well. As always, make sure each coat has thoroughly dried (about an hour) before adding the next.

6 For the final step, spread a bit of glue on the top side of the 1" (3 cm) metal pin back and press it firmly onto the back side of the lady. Set this aside until it is thoroughly dry.

Variation
on a Theme

Any figure or shape can be made into a beautiful and colorful pin. Use the same cut paper process to make this angel pin or any other shape. Marbled papers are perfect for an angel pin, given their ethereal swirls.

Bronze and Lace
Cuff Bracelet

The secret to this unusual bracelet is an acrylic transfer of the lace image, backed with silver foil to make it sparkle. To learn how to transfer the lace image, see How to Make Acrylic Transfers on page 155. Real lace under the tissue paper covering the bracelet gives texture to the surface of the piece and highlights the lace pattern. Brush a coat of glue over the brown tissue paper covering the cuff bracelet to give it a metallic sheen. To assure that the bracelet keeps its shape, the chipboard is backed with several pieces of wire.

Materials

Piece of ¹⁄₃₂" (.75 mm) chipboard or cardboard, 2" × 7" (5 cm × 18 cm)

31" (79 cm) of 22-gauge wire

Masking tape

Sheet of brown tissue paper

Small square of silver foil paper

Scissors

Pencil

Metallic gold marker

Ruler

PVA glue

Glue brush

Small dish of water

Acrylic transfer of a lace image

Piece of lace, 1" × 5" (3 cm x 13 cm)

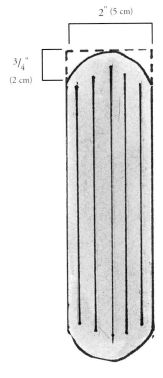

2" (5 cm)

3¹⁄₄" (2 cm)

Getting Started

Trim the corners of the chipboard to create an elongated oval shape as shown. Cut the wire into two lengths of 6 ¼" (16 cm), two lengths of 6" (15 cm), and one length of 6 ½" (17 cm). Use masking tape to secure the entire length of each piece of wire to the chipboard in the following order: 6" (15 cm), 6 ¼" (16 cm), 6 ½" (17 cm), 6 ¼" (16 cm), and 6" (15 cm). The side with these wires will be the inside of the bracelet.

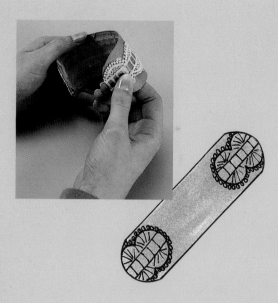

1 Cut two pieces of lace measuring 2 ¼" (6 cm) each and glue one down at each end of the oval chipboard, on the side without the wire, centering it between the long sides as shown in the illustration. Repeat with the other piece of lace on the other end. Gently bend the chipboard, wire side in, into a circular shape, being sure to leave at least a ¾" (2 cm) gap between the ends.

2 It is easier to work with the tissue if you thin the glue by dipping the glue brush in water before dipping it in the glue. Brush a thin coat of the glue and water mixture onto the surface of the bracelet. Lay down an 8" × 3" (20 cm × 8 cm) piece of tissue paper over the cuff, allowing it to slightly wrinkle and fold. Work it into the lace so that the pattern is clearly visible.

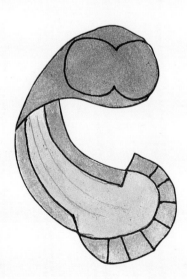

3 Clip the curves of the tissue paper extending beyond the edges of the chipboard as shown in the illustration. Brush a thin coat of glue around the inside edge of the bracelet and fold the tissue paper over to the inside. Make sure the tabs are pulled in firmly against the cardboard. Also be sure to fold in the long straight tabs on either side of the bracelet.

4 Cut a piece of tissue paper measuring 6 ½" × 1 ½" (17 cm × 4 cm) and round off the corners as you did the chipboard in step 1. Brush a thin coat of glue and water over the inside of the cuff and carefully lay the tissue paper into place. Brush a bit more glue and water over the entire surface of the cuff. This will give the cuff bracelet its metallic sheen.

5 Use the glue to secure the acrylic transfer to the silver foil and then carefully cut around the image of the lace. Glue this piece to the front of the cuff in the exact center.

6 From the edge of the tissue paper, cut two strips measuring ½" (1 cm) wide. Twist them together into a string as shown in the Origami Fold Bracelet step-by-step on page 184, and then glue the string around the edge of the lace acrylic transfer, framing the image. Trim off any excess string.

7 With the gold marker, draw a border all the way around the outside edge of the cuff. Draw over the outline of one piece of lace and, while the ink is still wet, smear it with your finger to give the cuff a weathered look. Repeat with the other piece of lace and the string frame around the transfer as well.

Variation
on a Theme

Cuff bracelets can take any shape or form; the basic construction remains the same. This puzzler takes its clues from the daily crosswords.

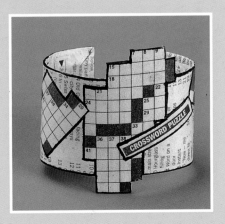

Floral Decoupage
Locket

My love for flowers became the subject of this elegant locket, but it is within the floral walls that the true value of this piece lies hidden: open the locket to reveal the silhouette of a very special person. To make the silhouette, a photograph of your subject becomes the pattern that you transfer using the carbon paper technique described in How to Transfer Images and Patterns on page 157. The solid color silhouette is reminiscent of an antique cameo and lends and heirloom air to the piece. For a more realistic approach, photocopy the photograph and cut out the image of your locket's featured character.

Materials

Needle-nosed pliers

Tweezers

Scissors

Small piece of $\frac{1}{16}$" (1.5 mm) chipboard or cardboard

PVA glue

Glue brush

Water-based polyurethane or acrylic medium

Masking tape

White paper for papier-mâché torn into strips

Papier-mâché paste mixed as directed on its package

Craft knife

Ruler

Pencil

Gold marker

2 gold 7 mm jump rings

Red tassel

Floral cutouts of images to decorate the locket

Yellow latex paint

Small paintbrush

Silhouette of a special friend cut out from heavy
  white paper

Embroidery needle

Getting Started

Out of the chipboard, cut two $1\frac{1}{2}$" (4 cm) squares and four triangular pieces, each $1\frac{1}{2}$" (4 cm) long and $\frac{3}{8}$" (1 cm) wide at the base. Cut out the pieces with the craft knife, using the ruler as a straight edge. Line up the ruler on the diagonal of each square, and use the knife to cut halfway through the thickness of the board from corner to corner. Cut only one diagonal on each square.

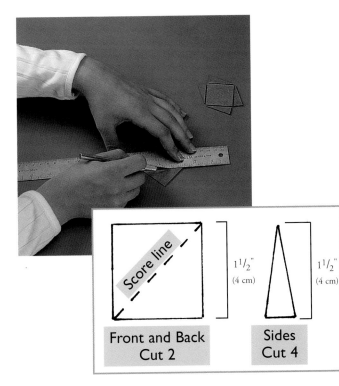

Score line

$1\frac{1}{2}$"
(4 cm)

$1\frac{1}{2}$"
(4 cm)

**Front and Back
Cut 2**

**Sides
Cut 4**

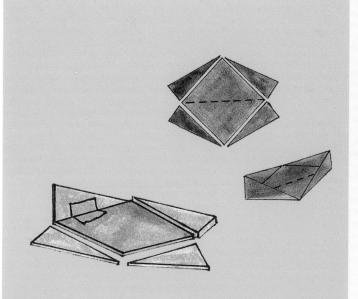

1 Lay the pieces out according to the illustration. One square piece should be placed scored side down, with the score traveling from left to right. Stand a triangle on its side edge, perpendicular to the adjoining edge of the square. Use the masking tape to secure it in place, taping it on both the inside and outside. Repeat with the three remaining triangles.

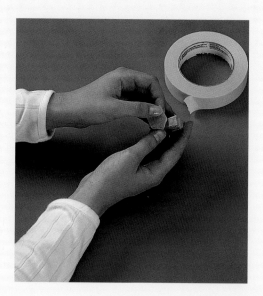

2 Gently fold the square along the score until the short edges of the adjacent triangles meet. Secure them in place with the masking tape. To complete the box, fold the second square over the top of the piece you just made, being sure that the score marks are pointed in the same direction for both squares. Fix the second square in place with tape.

3 Now that the skeleton of your locket is made, the "skin" must be created. With the white paper, apply three layers of papier-mâché over the box of the locket following the instructions given in How to Make Strip Papier-Mâché on page 139. Remember to allow each layer to dry a few hours before adding the next.

4 When the papier-mâché is thoroughly dry, orient the locket so that a corner of the square where two triangle points meet is situated at the top. Add the decoupage using the method described in How to Decoupage on page 155. When the glue is dry, apply five coats of either polyurethane or acrylic medium. As always, wait for each coat to dry before applying the next.

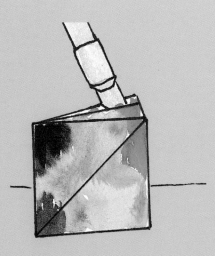

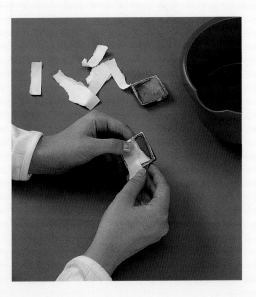

5 Use the knife to cut the locket in half all the way around the middle of the triangular sides. It may be helpful to first mark your cutting line lightly with pencil, and then place the locket on the edge on your work surface and cut it as you would a bagel.

6 Add a very neat layer of papier-mâché to the inside of the locket. When it is dry, brush on a coat of the yellow paint and then, when dry, a coat of polyurethane or acrylic medium.

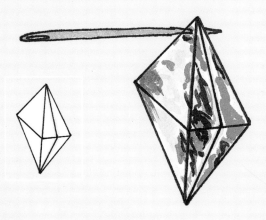

7 Hold the front and back of the locket in the "closed" position, and with the gold marker, draw a line on either side of the cut made earlier. Use the embroidery needle to punch a hole through the top point of the locket ⅛" (.3 cm) from the sides. Thread a jump ring through both the sides with the needle-nosed pliers. This ring will serve as the hinge for the locket.

8 In the bottom point of the front side only, punch another hole. Thread a jump ring through the hole and tie the tassel to the ring. Glue your silhouette inside the center back of the locket. String some silk cording or a favorite necklace through the hinge of the locket and try it on.

$\mathcal{T}$he playful creatures and fanciful designs created by paper folding and weaving have entertained generations. These two techniques can also make very modern objects of beauty and function, such as jewelry, that are surprisingly easy to make and durable.

Folding paper is not a complicated skill. However, to assure very neat and professional-looking results, use a ruler to take careful measurements. It also helps to pre-bend the fibers of the paper along the fold line, so that the fold will be placed accurately without any wrinkling or bunching. This is done by lining up the ruler between the two end points of the fold and running the blade of a butter knife between these points. The number of layers in the final piece is naturally increased as the paper is folded back on itself to create the desired pattern; this is what will give the jewelry its strength. The more layers of paper, the stronger the piece will be. For this reason, be careful when choosing the papers for your projects. A thick paper will not accept multiple folds and still give clean, neat, or accurate results.

Paper weaving is a wonderfully simple way to achieve a multi-colored and textural piece of art. The basic materials involve only some strips of paper to weave together. A portion of these strips is lined up side by side to create the warp of your weaving, traveling from top to bottom. The remaining strips of paper are the weft of the weaving and will travel horizontally over the first warp strip and under the next, continuing across the width of the piece in this pattern. The next weft (horizontal) strip does the opposite of the first, going under the first warp strip and over the next. The weaving gets its strength from the intersection of the warp and weft strips that gives a double layer of paper twice as strong as the original single thickness of paper.

Weaving and folding are both such simple techniques that you will quickly master them. What is so surprising is that such basic skills can produce a multitude of variations in pattern. With a little experimentation, you are sure to discover a wide variety of options to add to your design palette.

Woven and Folded Paper Jewelry

How to Basket Weave

▶ The basket weave is the most basic of weaving styles. Not only quick and easy, it is a beautiful design that has a multitude of variations.

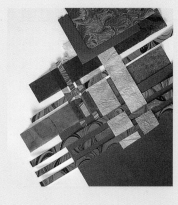

Materials

7 strips of pink paper

7 strips of yellow paper

Clipboard

I Line up the pink strips of paper, side by side, and slip their tops under the clip of the clipboard. These strips will make up the warp of your weaving.

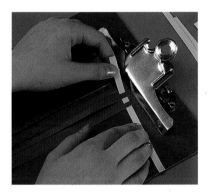

2 The yellow strips are the weft of your piece and will travel from right to left (or left to right). Starting with one, thread it under the first pink strip and over the next. Continue in this under/over pattern across the piece. Push the strip up against the clip of the board.

3 With another yellow strip, weave across the pink strips in the same under/over pattern, but this time start by going over the first pink strip. Push this piece firmly against the first strip you wove.

4 Repeat steps 2 and 3 for the length of the weaving.

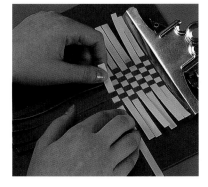

For neat, clean folds, it is important to pre-bend the fibers of the paper along the fold line. Follow these three easy steps, and you are sure to be pleased with the results of your paper folding project.

Materials

Ruler

Pencil

Butter knife

Folding paper project

I Carefully measure and mark off the endpoints of the fold on the side of the paper that will be hidden inside the final fold.

2 Line up the ruler between the two endpoints, and run the blade of the butter knife along its edge, creating an impression of a line.

3 Fold the paper over and crease it along the fold line you just made. Remember the fold line marked on the paper is always on the inside of the fold. For your work to progress efficiently, pre-bend the fibers along all the fold lines in the project before going back to fold them all.

Making the Jewelry

When I was little, I had an amazing folded paper hat that was made of newsprint with a big green and brown pheasant feather taped to the back of it. Most of us have made a folded paper hat, or boat, or fan at some point in our childhood. Some have had experience with origami or have made woven paper place mats. But paper folding and weaving need not end with childhood. Their artistic possibilities can extend through a lifetime.

Weaving and folding paper to make jewelry offer a wide assortment of creative options. To achieve multicolored variations of paper folding patterns laminate two different colored papers to each other. As you fold the paper, different colors will show. Try cutting slots into a folded piece so that another colored strip can be woven into the project. The variation of the Origami Fold Bracelet on page 185 simply has sections of the folded paper strip cut out to reveal the already existing second color laminated to the back.

You can vary the pattern of a basic basket weave by changing the number of warp strips the weft travels under or over in one pass. For example, weave under the first two warps strips and then over the next across the piece. Add texture by twisting the paper strips as you work , or by incorporating wire or ribbon.

Folding Tips

Folding, *combined* with a little bit of cutting, can create some playful pop-ups for lockets.

Cut out *portions* of a woven or folded piece to reveal other colors or images you affix to their backs.

Make small *origami* creatures to use for earrings, pendants, or charms.

After *folding* a number of paper strips into a patterned strap, weave these pieces together to create a colorful and/or textural visual.

Leave some *space* between each of the warp strips and each of the weft strips. These openings in the weaving will give the piece a lacy look.

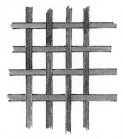

For *weavings* with a more earthy look, tear your strips instead of giving them a neatly cut edge.

Golden Braid
Choker

This choker is not only beautiful, but you can make it quickly and with ease. The gold foil accents the yellow and peach in the tie-dyed paper I found at my local art supply store. Braid it just as you would braid hair, except you are working with flat, two-dimensional pieces that need to be folded and creased as you weave them together. To make wearing this choker more comfortable, it is lined with interfacing that can easily be found in fabric or craft stores. Follow the illustrations and you will soon be wearing this piece yourself.

Materials

Piece of gold foil paper, 4" × 20"
(10 cm × 51 cm)

Piece of tie-dyed peach paper, 3" × 20"
(8 cm × 51 cm)

1" (3 cm) gold choker clip

PVA glue

Ruler

Scissors

Piece of interfacing, ¾" × 14" (2 cm × 36 cm)

Pliers

Pencil

Fold the gold foil paper in half,
with the glue on the inside.

Getting Started

Brush a thin coat of glue on the back side of the gold
paper and fold it in half lengthwise so that the piece
now measures 2" × 20" (5 cm × 51 cm). Firmly press
the two sides together, making sure that there are no
air bubbles. Cut three ½" × 20" (1 cm × 51 cm) strips
from this piece. Cut six ⅜" × 20" (1 cm × 51 cm) strips
from the peach paper.

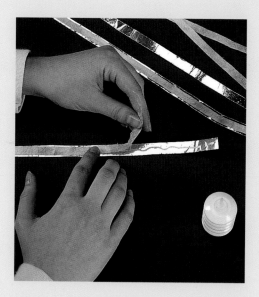

1 Run a thin bead of glue down the middle of one gold strip and lay a peach piece onto the glue, making sure that it is centered. Flip the piece over and glue another peach piece to the other side. Repeat with the remaining gold and peach strips.

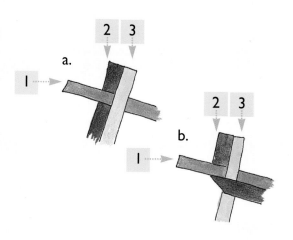

2 Lay the three pieces out according to the illustration, and braid them together by folding each strip forward as shown. So that it is easier to understand the illustrations, each strip is represented by a different color even though all three strips are peach. Begin by folding strip number 2 over to the right so that it is parallel to strip number 1.

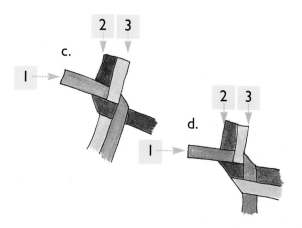

3 Next, fold strip number 1 to the left so that it runs parallel to strip number 3. Then strip number 3 is folded over to run parallel to strip number 2. Continue in this manner for the length of the strips.

4 Apply glue to one side of the braid and center the interfacing onto it.

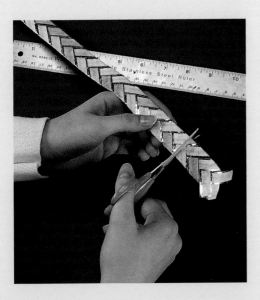

5 Use the scissors to cut off just enough of one end of the braid to have a nice clean and square edge. From that edge, measure off 12" (30 cm) and cut the braid. The choker clasp is adjustable, so the 12" (30 cm) measurement should fit most people.

6 Insert one end of the braid into one side of the choker clip, and use the pliers to bend the clip into place so it grips the paper. Repeat with the other end of the braid and the other side of the clip.

Variation
on a Theme

Colored paper string instead of strips of paper is braided to create this beautiful choker. The quantity of the paper strings used assures the strength and durability for a long-lasting treasure.

Origami Fold
Bracelet

This bold and colorful bracelet is not only decorative but remarkably functional. It is beautiful as a bracelet, yet due to its multiple layers of folds, it is sturdy enough to thread a watch onto and use as a watchband. You can also lengthen the pattern for the bracelet so that it may be used as an anklet or choker, or shorten the strap to decorate the face of a barrette. An entire ensemble of paper jewelry, requiring materials no more common than white paper and tissue paper, could be designed around this easily created strap bracelet.

Materials

Piece of green tissue paper, 1½" × 12"
 (4 cm × 30 cm)

Piece of blue tissue paper, 1½" × 12"
 (4 cm × 30 cm)

Piece of white copy paper or bond paper,
 1½" × 12" (4 cm × 30 cm)

Full sheet of purple tissue paper

PVA glue

Glue brush

Clipboard

Ruler

Craft knife

Water-based polyurethane

Small paintbrush

2 silver 7 mm jump rings

Silver bracelet clasp

Needle-nosed pliers

Butter knife

Embroidery needle

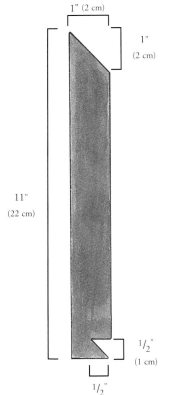

1" (2 cm)

1"
(2 cm)

11"
(22 cm)

½"
(1 cm)

½"
(1 cm)

Getting Started

Brush a coat of glue over one side of the white paper
and lay the green tissue paper on top of it. Flip the piece
over and do the same with the blue tissue paper. Follow
the illustrations to cut the paper into the needed shape for
the bracelet. Brush a single coat of polyurethane over each
side of the piece and set it aside to dry for approximately
one hour.

1 From the long side of the purple tissue paper, cut two strips of paper measuring ½" (1 cm) wide, and, starting at one end, twist each tightly so that each forms a thin string.

2 Hold the ends of each string together and slip them under the clip of the clipboard. Twist each string so tightly that it starts to curl back on itself. Then, hold the two free ends of the strings together and twist them in the opposite direction that you originally twisted them. Remove this double string from the clipboard and brush a coat of polyurethane over it. Set it aside to dry.

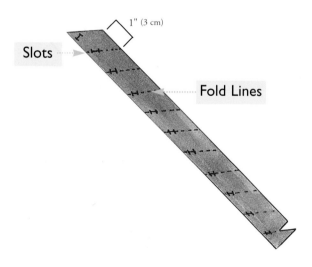

1" (3 cm)

Slots

Fold Lines

3 Once the green and blue piece is dry, mark off the paper in intervals of 1" (3 cm) as shown. Use the ruler and the butter knife to connect the marks as described earlier. This will crease the fibers so that it will be easier to fold the paper. Finally, use the craft knife to cut the slots in the paper according to the illustration.

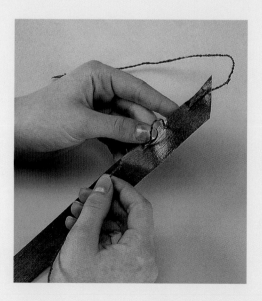

4 Hold the piece in front of you, blue side up. Starting at the pointed end, thread the purple string up from the back and down through the next slot in the paper. Continue in this manner for the length of the strip.

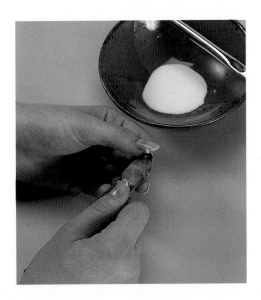

5 Place the piece in front of you, blue side up again, and fold along the first bend line so that the green side is now showing. Fold the paper back along the second fold line so that the blue side is showing again. Continue in this manner for the length of the strip. Use a bit of glue to secure all the folds in place.

6 Cut the ends of the purple string so that it extends only ¼" (.5 cm) beyond the edge of the strip. On both ends of the paper, fold the blue point back, capturing the end of the purple string in the fold. Glue the ends in place.

7 Use the needle to punch a hole in the point at each end of the bracelet. Thread a jump ring through each hole with the needle-nosed pliers, and then attach the clasp to one of the jump rings.

Variation on a Theme

This strap bracelet, folded exactly the same way as the one in the project, features cutouts that are removed to reveal overlapping colors.

Pinwheel *Earrings*

These pinwheels may appear to be fragile, but they are not too delicate to touch or to wear because they are made of thick, sturdy wallpaper. Wallpaper stores will frequently give away books of samples when a line of paper is discontinued or sold out. Wallpaper designed for the kitchen or bath is vinyl and therefore already water-proofed. This eliminates the need to coat the pinwheels with polyurethane without compromising the durability of the earrings.

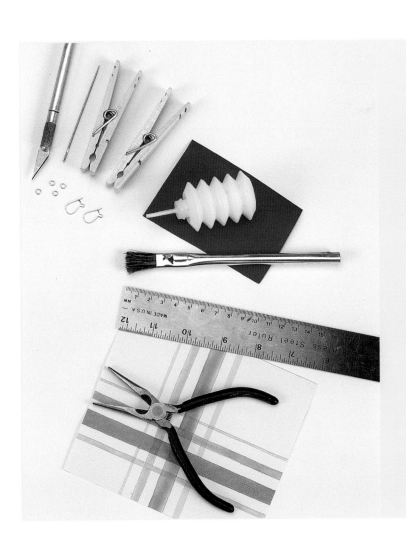

Materials

Piece of plaid wallpaper, 9" × 5" (23 cm × 13 cm)

PVA glue

Glue brush

Ruler

Craft knife

4 silver 4 mm jump rings

2 kidney wire earring hooks

2 clothespins

Embroidery needle

Needle-nosed pliers

Getting Started

Cut out two squares of the section of the plaid where the warp and the weft lines intersect and two squares of the white paper from between the plaid strips, each measuring at least 1½" (4 cm) square. Glue a white square and a plaid square back to back. Press down firmly to assure that there are no air bubbles. Repeat with the other two squares.

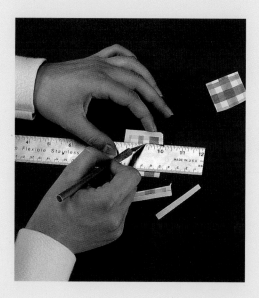

1 Trim each square of wallpaper so that it measures exactly 1½" (4 cm) across. Repeat with the other section of square wallpaper.

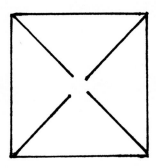

2 Use the ruler and the craft knife to cut each square along the lines shown in the illustration.

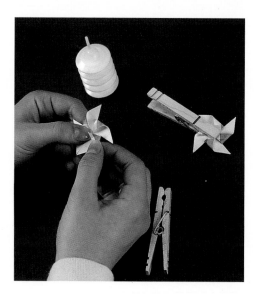

3 The white side of the square will be the inside of the pinwheel. Place a dot of glue in the center of this square, fold a corner into the middle and hold it in place. Continue adding a dot of glue and folding in every other corner until four have been glued in place. Use a clothespin to hold the corners in place while the glue dries, about one hour. Repeat with the other square of paper.

4 Once the glue has dried, use the needle to punch a hole in one point of each pinwheel, as shown.

5 With the needle-nosed pliers, thread a jump ring through the hole of one pinwheel, and then link another ring to the first. Repeat with the other pinwheel.

6 To finish off the earrings, simply slip one pinwheel onto each kidney wire earring back.

Variation on a Theme

The pinwheels are a fun form to play with, and you can easily adapt them to a number of earring styles. This pair of earrings puts smaller pinwheels onto post earring backs.

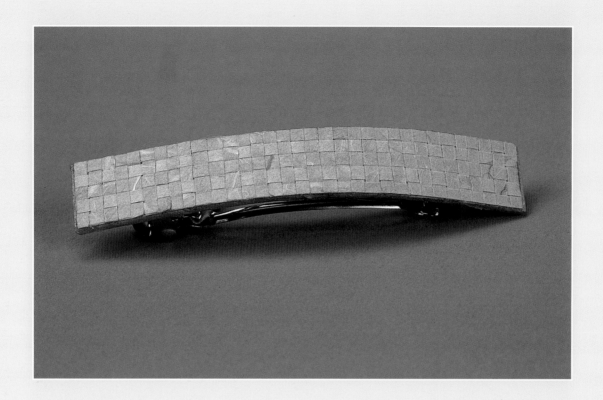

Basket Weave
Barrette

As school children, many of us made basket weave place mats from various colors of

construction paper. The same method used to make those childhood mats is the basis for

this fashionable barrette. The narrow strips of paper in muted colors give the barrette a

refined look. It is so easy to make, it will seem like child's play, but the result is a mature

personal accessory that will endure for years.

Materials

Barrette clip

Piece of $\frac{1}{16}$" (2 mm) chipboard or cardboard, $\frac{5}{8}$" × 4" (2 cm × 10 cm)

Piece of purple paper, 6 $\frac{1}{2}$" × 5" (17 cm × 13 cm)

Piece of green paper, 6 $\frac{1}{2}$" × 5" (17 cm × 13 cm)

PVA glue

Glue brush

3 clothespins

Clipboard

Ruler

Pencil

Scissors or craft knife

Embroidery needle

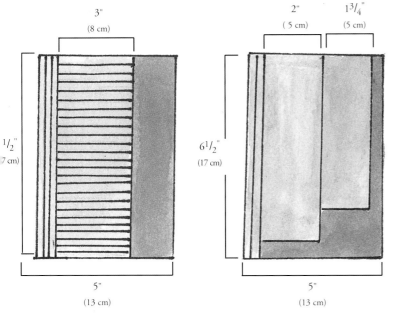

Getting Started

Begin by following the pattern to cut all the pieces of paper required to make this project. From the purple paper you need 3 strips measuring $\frac{1}{8}$" × 6 $\frac{1}{2}$" (.3 cm × 17 cm) and 32 strips measuring $\frac{1}{8}$" × 3" (.3 cm × 8 cm). From the green paper you need two strips measuring $\frac{1}{8}$" × 6 $\frac{1}{2}$" (.3 cm × 17 cm), a 2" × 6" (5 cm × 15 cm) piece, and a 5" × 1 $\frac{3}{4}$" (13 cm × 5 cm) piece. Line up the five long strips of paper side by side, starting with a purple strip and alternating colors. Slip the first $\frac{1}{2}$" (1 cm) of the ends of the paper beneath the clipboard clip.

1 The five long strips will be the warp of your weaving. With all of the short strips for the weft, use the basic basket weave technique described in How to Basket Weave on page 175 to create the decorative woven portion of the barrette. Use the tip of the needle to push the narrow strips close to each other, and be sure to center the weft strips on the warp.

2 Spread a thin coat of glue over one side of the piece of green paper measuring 2" × 6" (5 cm × 15 cm). Carefully remove the woven piece from the clipboard, and, making sure that it stays square, lay it into the glue on top of the green paper. Gently press the woven strips into the glue to assure that there are no air bubbles.

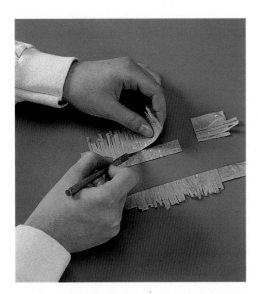

3 You will notice that there is about ³⁄₄" (2 cm) of unwoven weft strips on either side of the weaving and a bit of the warp strips overhanging the top and bottom. Using the craft knife, trim the unwoven portion so the piece measures ⁵⁄₈" × 4" (2 cm × 10 cm). This is the decorative face of the barrette.

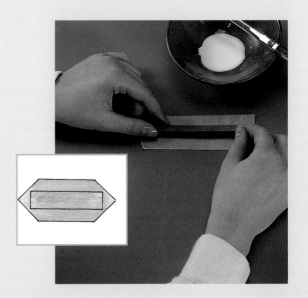

4 To make the barrette base, spread a thin coat of glue on one side of the chipboard, and, making sure that it is centered, press it firmly glue side down onto the 5" × 1³⁄₄" (13 cm × 5 cm) green paper. Trim the corners of the green paper as shown in the illustration. Leave ¹⁄₈" (.3 cm) of paper showing beyond the corner of the board, so the edge will be completely covered.

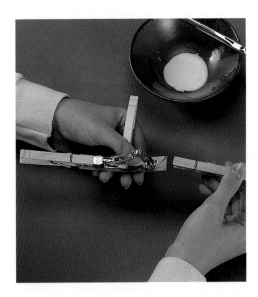

5 Brush a thin coat of glue onto the exposed paper around the board and fold the two short edges tightly up and over the board. Continue by folding the two longer sides up and over the board in the same fashion, paying special attention to the corners. Use either your fingers or the point of the needle to tuck in the corners as you would when wrapping a present.

6 Apply a generous coat of PVA glue to the top side of the barrette clip. Center the paper-covered board over the clip and use a clothespin to secure the centers of each to the other. Gently bend the board to the curve of the clip using a clothespin to hold each end in place. Leave the three pins securing the piece while the glue dries, about one hour.

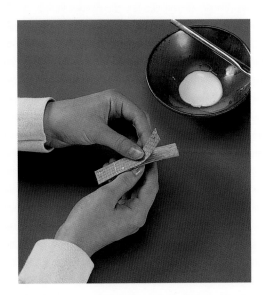

7 Once the glue holding the paper-covered board to the clip has dried, brush a thin coat of PVA over the top of the board and carefully lay the woven piece in place. Press it firmly but gently into the glue, making sure there are no air bubbles.

Variation
on a Theme

Simply changing the shape of the board is an easy way to achieve a whole new look for the barrette. This diamond-shaped barrette also includes twice as many colors as the previous project.

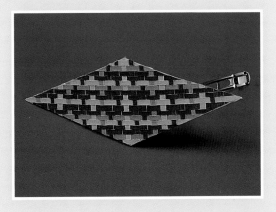

How to Make Paper

Making paper is fun, easy, and rewarding, and requires only a few household items, some scraps of paper, and various art supplies. This recipe produces beautiful navy-colored paper, but you can create a different colored paper simply by substituting the blue dye with another color; or after you have made a few blue sheets of paper, add some yellow or red dye to the pulp to produce either green or purple sheets of paper. For a personal touch, experiment with different paper types, or add objects such as petals or lace to the pulp. Once you discover how quickly you can create beautiful paper, you will find yourself with a growing stack of unique papers to use for countless creative projects.

Materials

Paper scraps

Blender

Water

Blue dye

Large, shallow vat (large enough to contain deckle and mold)

8½" × 11" (22 cm × 28 cm) deckle and mold

2 pieces of felt just larger than the paper you are making

Pressing boards

Sheet of foam core or other smooth surface

Towels and sponges

Bucket

Putty or butter knife

1
Tear the paper into small pieces, measuring no more than 1" (3 cm) square, and place them in the bucket. Add enough water to cover the paper and let it soak overnight to soften the fibers. The next day, put a small handful of the paper pieces into the blender with a little bit of water and blend until the pulp is smooth (it should resemble the consistency of cooked oatmeal). Repeat until all of the soaked paper bits have been made into pulp. Pour into the shallow vat and add several tablespoons of blue dye until you have created a rich, blue mixture.

2
Mix enough water into the pulp so that it has a soupy consistency (the more water you add to the pulp, the thinner the sheet of paper will be). Agitate the mixture to ensure an even dispersion of the pulp. Stack the mold on top of the deckle and, beginning at one side of the vat, slip the deckle and mold beneath the surface of the pulp solution in one smooth movement.

3

Lift the deckle and mold straight up out of the vat and gently shake them to ensure an even dispersion of the paper pulp. Allow as much water as possible to drain off, and remove the mold from the top of the deckle.

4

To prevent the pulp from sticking to the felts, soak them in water and then wring them out. Place one pressing board on the work surface with a piece of felt on top of it. In a quick, smooth motion flip the deckle over onto the felt so that the sheet of paper you are forming is trapped between the screen of the deckle and the felt. With a towel or sponge, press against the screen of the deckle to squeeze out as much water from the pulp sheet as possible. Gently remove the deckle, leaving the pulp sheet on the felt. If the pulp starts to tear as you lift off the deckle, press out more water before continuing.

5

Lay the other felt on top of the pulp sheet and the other pressing board on top of that. Press the sheet firmly between the two boards to remove more water. You may find that standing on the boards is the easiest way to do this. Carefully remove the top board and felt.

6

Lift the felt that the sheet of paper is on and turn it over onto the foam core, pulp side down. Press the sheet against the foam core and gently peel the felt away from the sheet of paper. If the paper starts to tear, press it back against the foam to remove more moisture before continuing to peel off the felt. Leave the newly formed sheet of paper on the foam for several hours to dry.

7

When the edges of the paper sheet start to pull away from the foam core, and the center of the sheet feels dry to the touch, slip a putty or butter knife between the paper and the foam core, and gently pry the paper from the surface.

Paper-Making Tips

1 To make your own deckle and mold set, use two matching picture frames and window screening (available at any hardware store) to cover the opening of one frame. Remove the glass, backing, and stands from the frames so that only the front portion of the frame remains. Wrap the screening around one frame and staple or glue it in place. This frame is now the deckle. Stack the other frame on top of the deckle to use it as the mold for your paper.

2 Use cookie cutters as molds on top of a deckle to make small, fun shaped pieces of paper to use for invitations or name tags.

3 Make larger sheets of paper by lining up and slightly overlapping multiple sheets of the unpressed, wet paper on a large pressing board and then press them all at once to form a bigger composite piece of paper.

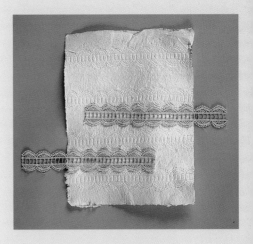

Working with Metals
and Alternative Materials

Gold, the noble metal that can withstand time and the
elements, has a long tradition in the history of jewelry.
To continue, extend, and enrich the tradition and to
become part of that history is a compelling impetus for the
contemporary jeweler.

designing in gold

The physical properties
of gold—its beauty, malleability, and preciousness—
challenge the artist to create work that transcends fashion
and trend. Each of the four artists in this chapter, working
in a highly distinctive personal style, has accepted that
challenge.

The preciousness of gold is a powerful metaphor
for Barbara Heinrich and contributes to the spiritual
dimension of her work. Her goldwork is distinguished by
textures in which a softly glowing matte *skin* of 24-karat
gold is illuminated by selective hand burnishing.

In her current goldwork, Kathe Timmerman retains the same playfulness and fluidity that characterized her colorful aluminum mesh jewelry. Although her palette has narrowed, Timmerman uses different surface finishes to describe her jewelry forms.

For Michael Good, gold is the perfect material—it is beautiful, malleable, and superbly suited to the specialized metalsmithing technique that yields his signature jewelry forms. He can work quite thin sheets of gold into hollow forms that have both strength and lightness. He polishes the gold to a high, reflective finish that also emphasizes his fluid design.

Gold is part of the palette of metals that Abrasha uses to construct his perfectly engineered forms. His jewelry is decidedly contemporary in its minimalist design and in its contrast of materials. Gold, brought to a softly brushed finish with burnished highlights, is the warm note among cool sterling silver, platinum, and stainless steel.

ABRASHA
NECKLACE
18-karat gold and diamonds
Fabricated

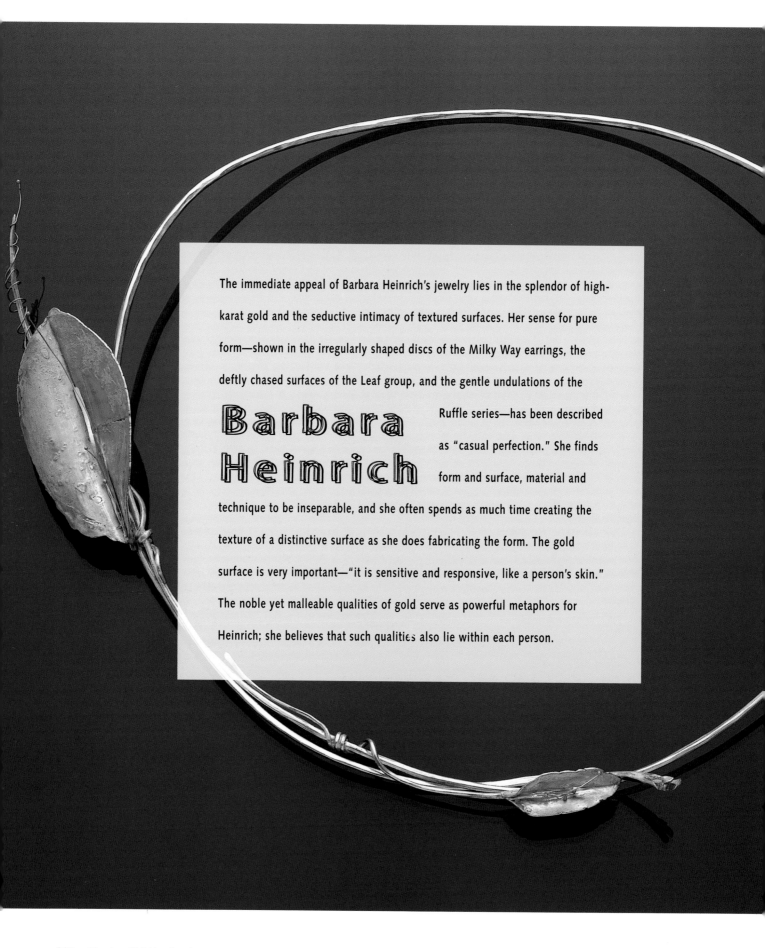

The immediate appeal of Barbara Heinrich's jewelry lies in the splendor of high-karat gold and the seductive intimacy of textured surfaces. Her sense for pure form—shown in the irregularly shaped discs of the Milky Way earrings, the deftly chased surfaces of the Leaf group, and the gentle undulations of the

Barbara Heinrich

Ruffle series—has been described as "casual perfection." She finds form and surface, material and technique to be inseparable, and she often spends as much time creating the texture of a distinctive surface as she does fabricating the form. The gold surface is very important—"it is sensitive and responsive, like a person's skin." The noble yet malleable qualities of gold serve as powerful metaphors for Heinrich; she believes that such qualities also lie within each person.

Heinrich's jewelry joins the jewelry-making traditions of two countries. By the time she came to the United States to study, she had been formally apprenticed to a goldsmith in Germany for three years and had studied at the Fachhoch-schule für Gestaltung in Pforzheim. In the graduate metals program at Rochester Institute of Technology, Heinrich took an experimental approach to material (working with aluminum and plastic) and to design (concentrating on personal expression).

When she set up her studio, Heinrich combined the two educational experiences. Disciplined technique and creative design allow her complete freedom to express her artistic vision in gold. She seeks to create timeless classics whose aesthetic qualities endure just as gold does.

BROOCH *Leaf*
18-karat gold and diamonds
Hammer-textured and formed

NECKLACE *Leaf*
18-karat gold and sterling silver
Forged and constructed

Specific inspirations are often the impulse for a new body of work. Fairy tales, painting, forms found in nature, music, prayer, or simply daydreaming—anything that touches me deeply—can set off the creative process. I prepare myself by keeping a sketchbook at hand.

The Ruffle series started with the underlying image of a flower opening up. In some of my earlier jewelry, such as the Milky Way group, the reference

technique was clear. Now I do not want the design to be too narrative or too specific. I want to capture the substance of the inspiration, the beauty of the image—but the form must speak on its own.

After developing a clear idea of what I want the piece to look like, I then consider the most direct way to make it. I develop forming and texturing techniques to suit the design and the material. The Ruffle Pendant is fabricated in 18-karat red gold, quite a hard alloy, that comes from Germany. I roll the

RING   *Diamond*
18-karat gold and diamonds
Constructed

metal between sheets of paper to give it a matte surface. I like to make the jewelry the way I draw it; thus, when I saw out the disc shape, I do not want a perfect circle. I hammer the edges to thicken them, and then dome the discs in a wood dapping block with wood punches. The gold is thin enough to "ruffle" with forming pliers, but still thick enough to resist warping. I repeat the process of bending with pliers and gently flattening the disc several times, until the ruffles form a casual, random pattern. I nest the two cups and solder them together, and then solder a short stem of twisted gold wire to the center.

I finish the surface with powdered pumice, applied with a toothbrush and water. I heat the gold gently with the torch and pickle it in acid, a technique called depletion gilding, to create a layer of fine gold. I contrast the soft, warm glow of this matte surface with the hard shine of the hand-burnished edge. This selective highlighting illuminates the surface and defines the form. Finally, I epoxy a freshwater pearl to the wire stem, and the pendant is complete.

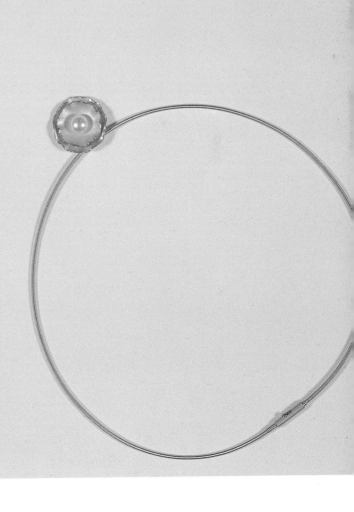

BROOCHES
18-karat gold and opal
Hammer-textured and constructed

BRACELET *Leaf*
18-karat gold and diamonds
Chased and constructed

barbara heinrich

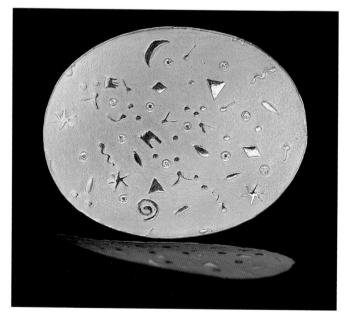

EARRINGS, PENDANT, BROOCH, RING
Ruffle Group
18-karat gold and freshwater pearls
Constructed

BROOCH
Milky Way
18-karat gold
and diamond
Embossed
and construc

BROOCH AND EARRINGS
18-karat gold and tourmaline cabochons
Hammer-textured and forged

BROOCH   *Opal*
18-karat gold and boulder opal
Hammer-textured and constructed

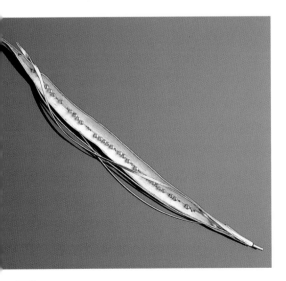

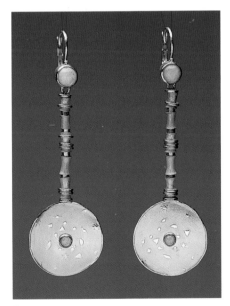

PIN
18-karat gold, sterling silver, and cultured
gray pearls
Forged and constructed

EARRINGS   *Milky Way*
18-karat gold and opals
Embossed, forged, and constructed

RINGS
18-karat gold, colored sapphires,
diamonds, and pearl
Textured and constructed

An interest in women's experience and history, particularly the image of women in nineteenth-century novels and in contemporary fashion, informs Kathe Timmerman's approach to jewelry design. She journeyed through Australia, Asia, the Middle East, and Europe before entering the metal-

Kathe Timmerman

smithing program at San Diego State University. Whimsical forged jewelry and raised sculptural vessels formed the focus of her student work.

Timmerman introduced a collection of aluminum mesh jewelry in her first production line. The fine-gauge screen, anodized to brilliant hues, captured silver and gold foil in its grid. The mesh, recalling the transparency of lingerie, formed easily. The color-and-texture collage

compositions, inspired by the work of

Jean Arp, were framed in silver, which

provided structural support for the mesh.

The relatively low cost

of the material allowed

Timmerman to play.

Her collection has

grown in new directions,

adding silver and gold ear-

rings, rings, and bracelets

in simple sculpted forms. Timmerman's

sense of fun shows in the way that rings and

bracelets wrap informally around the finger

or wrist, gracefully enhancing the natural

contours of the body.

PIN
Aluminum mesh with gold, silver,
and copper foils, and sterling silver
Anodized and die-formed

RRINGS   *Magic Carpet Ride*
rling silver, 24-karat vermeil, aluminum mesh
h gold, silver, and copper foils, and pearls
med and fabricated

Recently I have designed a line of gold jewelry with the goal of making it as playful as my work in mesh. As these designs have become more fluid and more sophisticated, I have refined my technique. I shape the abstract forms to suggest exotic flowers, such as orchids.

Though I like to work with Ceylon sapphires and black pearls, metal is always primary. I form it to embrace the stone, which provides color and contrasts with the gold. I sometimes combine different surface finishes—the matte surface of glass-bead-blasted gold with the reflective finish of tumbled gold—to complement the convex and concave shapes in

technique

the jewelry. Often, I construct paper models from my sketches before working the metal. But if the mental image is clear enough, I work with the metal

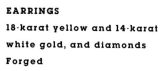

EARRINGS
18-karat yellow and 14-karat
white gold, and diamonds
Forged

immediately. I use both production techniques (including die-forming) and labor-intensive hand-forming techniques (such as working with a mallet over small anvil heads and form-ing blocks).

Whereas mesh only suggested the possibility of sculptural form, the work in silver and gold is more three-dimensional, more fully realized, and more resolved. The natural environment of the seashore and the voluptuous forms of the female and the flower inspire my design.

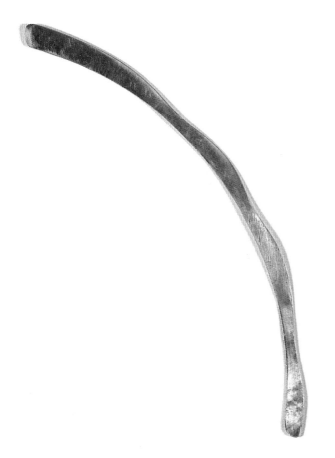

EARRINGS *Mesh*
Sterling silver and 24-karat vermeil
Formed

EARRINGS *Spiral*
Aluminum mesh with gold and copper foils, and sterling silver
Anodized

EARRINGS
18-karat gold
Forged

kathe timmerman

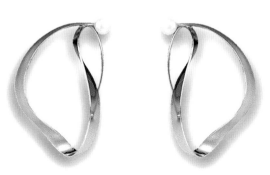

EARRINGS
Sterling silver and 24-karat vermeil
Formed and forged

STICKPINS
Gold, sterling silver, and ivory
Forged and fabricated

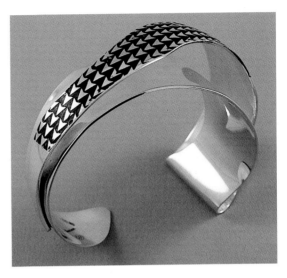

BRACELET
Sterling silver and copper
Formed and photo-etched

RING AND EARRINGS
14-karat and 18-karat gold, 24-karat vermeil, and sapphire
Formed and forged

PENDANT
18-karat yellow gold and 14-karat white gold,
and Australian opal
Forged

Self-taught jeweler Michael Good started working in 1968. His first designs were simple flat shapes with hammered surfaces, cut from thin sheets of 14-karat gold. Then he began to experiment with ways to make the gold

Michael Good

sheet three-dimensional by hammering the material into hollow forms. But it was not until he was introduced to the work of the influential teacher and metalsmith Heikki Seppä, with his new approach to hammer raising, that Good had the technical means to realize his vision of a fluid, dynamic line moving gracefully through space.

Good found the perfect union of concept and technology. He could hammer and form his flat metal pattern with a cross peen hammer over specially designed sinusoidal stakes, using Seppä's anticlastic raising technique, to create hollow "shell" forms. Within his design vocabulary, any form was now theoretically possible.

Good reinterpreted and refined Seppä's ideas for the scale of jewelry. The success of Good's signature jewelry forms relies on his ability to "move" metal. That is, working with hammer and stake to finesse the flat sheet into a stable, hollow, three-dimensional structure.

RINGS
Knot, HPE, and Double Loop©
18-karat yellow gold
Anticlastic raised

NDANT
irit Sun Pendant with Spirit Sun Diamond©
karat yellow gold and diamond
ticlastic raised

technique

My designs are directly related to the material and the technique I use. The anticlastic forming process determines the aesthetics of the piece. It takes away all the extraneous things; there is no soldering, no clasps.

Each piece begins with a sheet of 18-karat gold, on which the pattern is drawn. For each new design, a flat pattern is developed, then hammered into an anticlastic form. I alter the flat pattern until I finally reach the three dimensional form as I want it to be. Making the prototype is the most exciting part. That is the heart of it.

To take the flat sheet to a dimensional, hollow structure involves forming the metal. The shape of the tool determines the shape of the finished piece.

PENDANT
18-karat yellow gold
Anticlastic raised

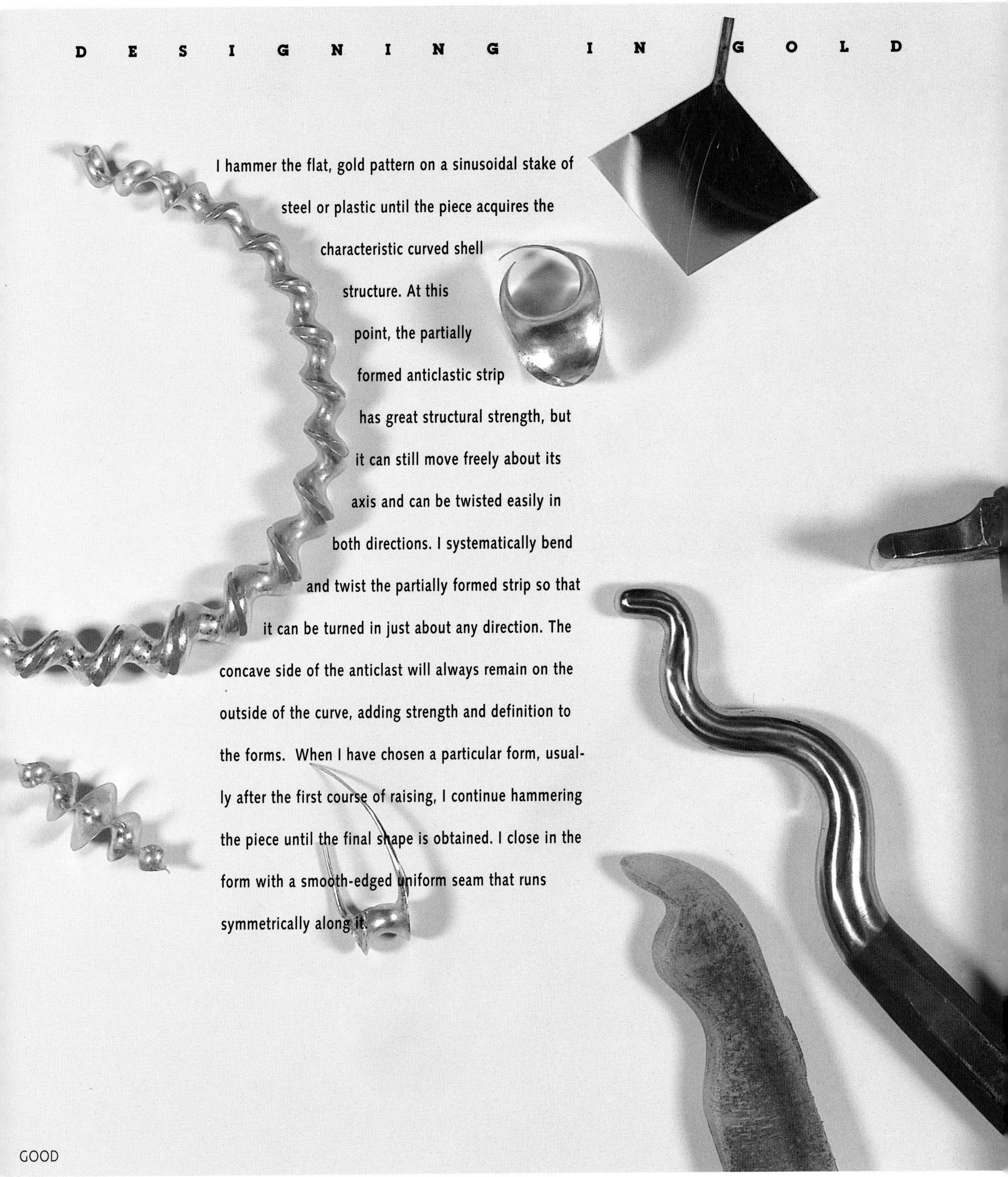

I hammer the flat, gold pattern on a sinusoidal stake of

steel or plastic until the piece acquires the

characteristic curved shell

structure. At this

point, the partially

formed anticlastic strip

has great structural strength, but

it can still move freely about its

axis and can be twisted easily in

both directions. I systematically bend

and twist the partially formed strip so that

it can be turned in just about any direction. The

concave side of the anticlast will always remain on the

outside of the curve, adding strength and definition to

the forms. When I have chosen a particular form, usual-

ly after the first course of raising, I continue hammering

the piece until the final shape is obtained. I close in the

form with a smooth-edged uniform seam that runs

symmetrically along it.

GOOD

BRACELET   *Knot©*
18-karat yellow gold
Anticlastic raised

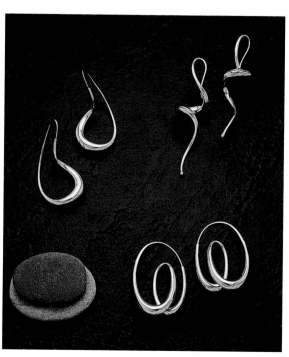

EARRINGS   *Figure Eight, Helicoidal, and Baroque©*
18-karat yellow gold
Anticlastic raised

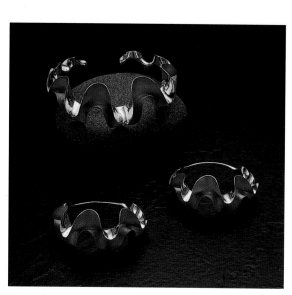

BRACELET AND EARRINGS   *Ruffle©*
18-karat yellow gold
Anticlastic raised

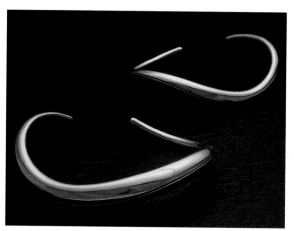

BRACELETS   *Light and Heavy Wave Cuff©*
18-karat yellow gold
Anticlastic raised

BRACELET   *Double Loop©*
18-karat yellow gold
Anticlastic raised

EARRINGS   *Single Loop©*
18-karat yellow gold
Anticlastic raised

PENDANT AND EARRINGS   *Zahna©*
18-karat yellow gold
Anticlastic raised

michael good

BRACELET
Triple Loop with Diamonds©
18-karat yellow gold and diamonds
Anticlastic raised

EARRINGS
Platinum Rolled Torque©
18-karat yellow gold
and platinum
Anticlastic raised

Austere, restrained, intellectual **are** words that describe the jewelry of Abrasha. No decorative details detract from the pristine geometric composition.

Abrasha

Yet this engineered perfection and sense of order reveal the unexpected: the contrast of materials, the logic of asymmetry.

Abrasha's decision to become a goldsmith was instantaneous. Visiting a jeweler's studio in his native Amsterdam, he was captivated by the tools and the mystique of the workshop. Convinced of his métier, he entered the Goldschmiedschule in Pforzheim, the historic center of the German jewelry industry.

Abrasha's apprenticeship as a model maker in a jewelry company introduced him to some of Germany's most influential innovators in design. He later worked as an assistant to the master goldsmith Klaus Ullrich. By the mid-1970s, Abrasha had arrived in San Francisco. He did bench work and eventually set up his own workshop. Gradually he began to execute his own designs and to develop his distinctive formal vocabulary.

Abrasha describes his design as industrial, cool, machinelike. His signature rivets, which connect materials that cannot be joined by soldering, fulfill the Bauhaus principle that form should follow function. Abrasha's jewelry forms—circles, spheres, and cones, punctuated by gold rivets, brilliant diamonds, or crisp edges—appeal to logic and reason. The rigidly

RING
18-karat gold, platinum,
and diamond
Fabricated

geometric square pin series explores material within clearly delineated design parameters.

Abrasha's jewelry speaks of discipline and control. Although the forms may seem cerebral, even cool, the beautiful and unexpected surfaces betray the hand of a sensitive artist. Rewarding close attention, his work yields the exquisite detail, the subtle refinement.

BRACELET
Stainless steel, 24-karat and 18-karat gold, and diamond
Machined and fabricated

The Bauhaus aesthetic, the Russian constructivists, and Japanese design sensibilities influence my work. The design process starts with an idea, then a quick sketch. My concern for precision, geometry, and balance leads to many possible variations of the original idea before I arrive at its final expression. For me, the design process had always been laborious and time-consuming: my German training dictated that I draw with ballpoint pen, with no erasures. Now, after the initial drawing, I move to the computer to quickly generate variations of measurement, scale, and proportion.

The finished drawing serves as a guideline for making the piece. During the working process, I make decisions at each step, thus refining the concept. I work in a restrained palette of materials: 18-karat and 24-karat gold, sterling silver, platinum, stainless steel, and diamonds. I am drawn to the rich yellow color of gold.

technique

CUFFLINKS AND TUXEDO STUDS
18-karat gold and diamonds
Fabricated

Silver, oxidized to a dark black, creates a wonderful foil for high-karat golds; the cold reflectivity of polished platinum provides a subtle contrast to round or square-cut diamonds; and stainless steel introduces an industrial, contemporary element.

By inclination and by training, I am a fabricator. I alloy 18-karat gold to make both sheet and wire by weighing out pure gold, fine silver, and copper, melting them in a crucible with my torch, and then pouring the molten metal into an ingot mold. I forge the billet and roll it to the desired thickness. I then lay out my design on the sheet gold, sawing and filing shapes almost to size. I use pliers, hammers, bending tools, punches, and doming blocks to achieve dimensional forms. I file the individual pieces yet again to exact measurement, and then fit parts together and solder them. If stainless steel is included, I drill holes for the rivets. I then set the stones and bring the surface to a soft, brushed finish, burnishing the edges and bezels. Then, finally, I join the stainless steel with 24-karat gold rivets.

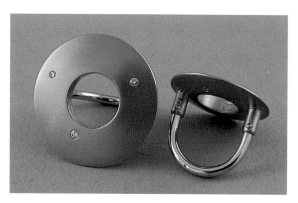

RINGS
18-karat gold, platinum, and diamonds
Fabricated

RING
18-karat gold,
platinum,
and diamonds
Fabricated

abrasha

PENDANT
18-karat gold and diamonds
Fabricated

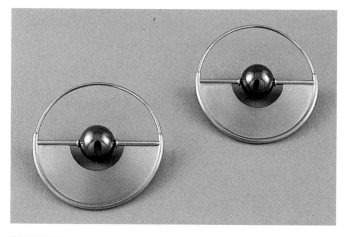

EARRINGS
18-karat gold, stainless steel, and hematite
Fabricated

EARRINGS
18-karat gold,
stainless steel,
and hematite
Fabricated

BRACELET
Stainless steel and 18-karat gold
Fabricated and cast

RING
18-karat gold
and stainless steel
Cast and fabricated

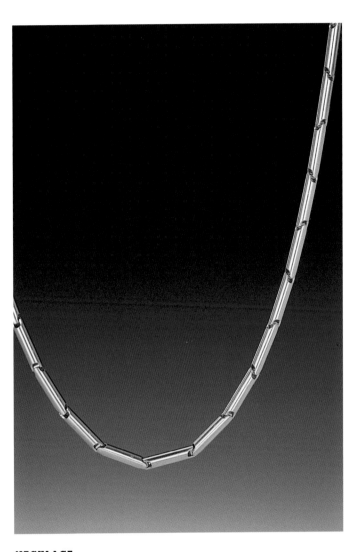

NECKLACE
Stainless steel and 18-karat gold
Machined, cast, and fabricated

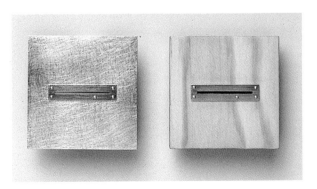

PINS   #5 and #6
Stainless steel, plywood, 18-karat gold, and sterling silver
Fabricated

Although a highly-developed personal aesthetic is evident in each of their jewelry, Reiko Ishiyama, Didi Suydam, and

Lorelei Hamm find common ground in their material of choice—silver. And, surprisingly, silver contributes to the artist's shared sculptural aesthetic, one that embraces both the organic and the geometric, and emphasizes structure and three-dimensional form.

Each artist uses traditional metalsmithing techniques to fabricate her jewelry. Both Suydam and Hamm's architectonic forms are hollow constructed, but Suydam replicates her prototypes by casting multiples, and Hamm prefers to individually fabricate all her work.

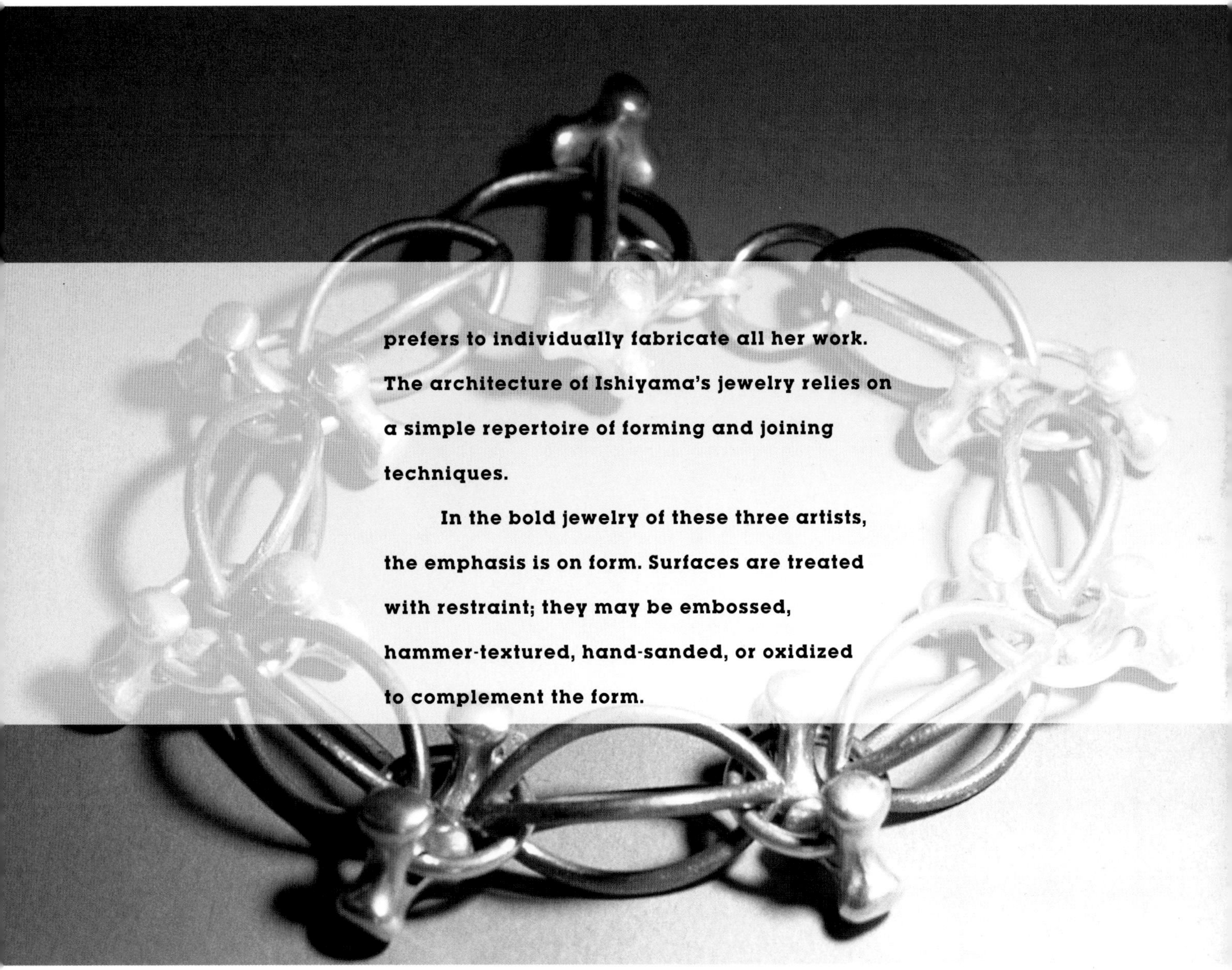

The architecture of Ishiyama's jewelry relies on

a simple repertoire of forming and joining

techniques.

In the bold jewelry of these three artists,

the emphasis is on form. Surfaces are treated

with restraint; they may be embossed,

hammer-textured, hand-sanded, or oxidized

to complement the form.

BRACELET
Stainless steel, 24-karat and 18-karat gold, and diamond
Machined and fabricated

LORELEI HAMM
BRACELET
Sterling silver
Cast and fabricated

Reiko Ishiyama remembers, as a young woman, watching a Japanese metalsmith forge a simple tool. She was fascinated that metal, which had always seemed so hard, could be soft and malleable. That private epiphany determined her course.

She became apprenticed to a metalsmith who specialized in objects for the Japanese tea

Reiko Ishiyama

ceremony. Eventually she moved into sculpture, working with welded copper, iron, and steel. Although conceptual art was popular in Japan in the late 1960s and 1970s, Ishiyama remained fascinated by the material—how it could be transformed in the artist's hands.

When she first arrived in New York in the mid-1980s, both her work space and range of tools were very limited. Working with only a jeweler's sawframe on a small tabletop, Ishiyama produced a collection of jewelry of remarkable freshness and spontaneity.

Architectural spaces, and the play of light and shadow they create, have inspired her design. In her earlier work, Ishiyama presented a form, sawed a path that followed its contour, and then gently pulled the flat shape into a three-dimensional shape. The pattern of light and shadow of such a piece has as strong a presence as the object itself. In her current bracelets, thin, narrow, undulating strips of metal recall the materials and techniques of basketry.

Ishiyama does not seek to completely control the metal, but rather to understand its qualities and possibilities. In both the organic

PINS
Sterling silver
Pierced and shaped; sandblasted finish

and the geometric forms, the artist's sense of touch is expressed through the softly textured surfaces, the crisp yet wavy edges, and the interesting dimensional quality of her pieces. Without dominating or overpowering the wearer, Ishiyama's jewelry has a strong aesthetic presence.

ACELETS
erling silver and gold plate
erced and shaped

Photography: James Dee

I don't usually begin by drawing or sketching, but rather by bending, shaping, hammering, or cutting pieces of silver. My designs evolve through working

technique

directly with the material. My hands are the ultimate source of my ideas—I develop a design and streamline the technical process through this way of working. Good pieces are a duet of material and technique: both are equally important for a design to be successful.

I use the jeweler's traditional tools and techniques (hammering, sawing, filing, and soldering) to achieve form. I choose surface textures to describe the form: silver might be sandblasted, hammered into a plate of pitted iron, or hand-finished with coarse sandpaper.

I work exclusively with silver and gold. The way silver reflects or absorbs light, depending upon its finish, captivates me; I also like how it ages, developing a

PINS
Sterling silver
Hammer-textured and shaped

Photo: James Dee

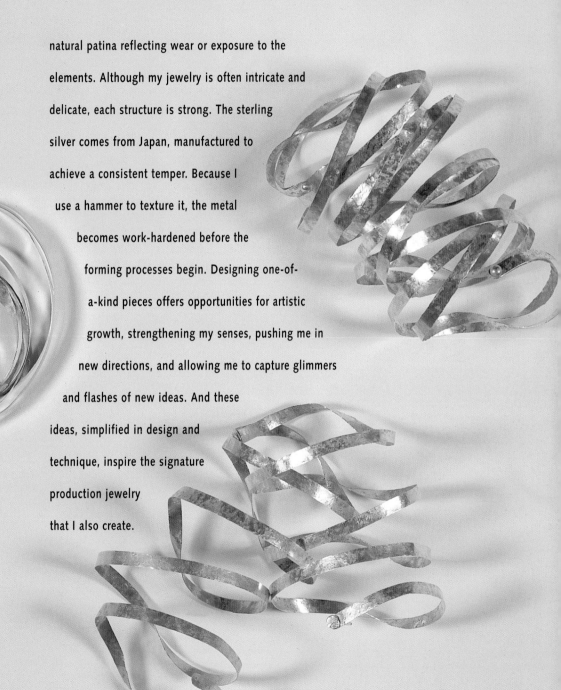

natural patina reflecting wear or exposure to the

elements. Although my jewelry is often intricate and

delicate, each structure is strong. The sterling

silver comes from Japan, manufactured to

achieve a consistent temper. Because I

use a hammer to texture it, the metal

becomes work-hardened before the

forming processes begin. Designing one-of-

a-kind pieces offers opportunities for artistic

growth, strengthening my senses, pushing me in

new directions, and allowing me to capture glimmers

and flashes of new ideas. And these

ideas, simplified in design and

technique, inspire the signature

production jewelry

that I also create.

EARRINGS
18-karat gold
Hammer-textured and formed

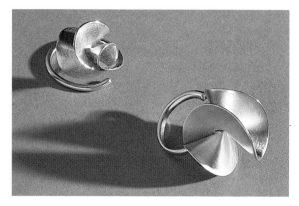

RINGS
Sterling silver and gold plate
Fabricated

BRACELETS
Sterling silver
Hammer-textured and constructed

PINS
Sterling silver and gold plate
Pierced and shaped

EARRINGS
Sterling silver and gold plate
Hammer-textured and formed

Photography: James Dee

BRACELETS
14-karat gold, sterling silver, and gold plate
Pierced, laminated, and formed

BRACELETS
Sterling silver and gold plate
Pierced and shaped

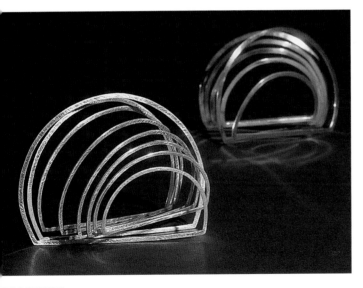

reiko ishiyama

BRACELETS
Sterling silver
Hammered and formed

EARRINGS
Sterling silver
Pierced and shaped; sandblasted finish

Didi Suydam entered Rhode Island School of Design intending to study sculpture. Although she soon switched to jewelry design, sculptural concerns continue to influence her work. Suydam interprets the body as landscape, and her jewelry as site-specific. Her bracelets,

Didi Suydam

earrings, and necklaces are meant to move, to sway, and to be felt, physically and visually. Her work harmonizes with the natural rhythms and contours of the body.

A semester spent studying in Rome had a profound impact on Suydam. Her jewelry resonates with associations to ancient artifacts, architectural and natural forms, and formal geometry.

Although Suydam makes a clear distinction between her impressive one-of-a-kind jewelry and her elegant production jewelry, they share a common aesthetic and sense of form. She makes a lot of drawings to establish her forms. Then she simplifies them, reconfiguring proportion, rhythm, and repetition. She must visualize shapes: how they work together, how to construct them, and how to make them function as jewelry. She finds the problem-solving nature of production design both challenging and satisfying.

BRACELET
Sterling silver and commercial chain
Cast and textured

EARRINGS
Sterling silver and gold plate
Cast, textured, and oxidized

PENDANTS   *Vessel*
Sterling silver, gold plate, and commercial chain
Cast and oxidized

Silver suits the proportion and scale of my jewelry. To achieve dimensional

form, I fabricate the metal, using traditional hollow construction techniques:

scoring and folding, and forming with hammers, stakes, and small dapping

punches. In designing for production, I seek solutions, not compromises. How

can I make a piece as quickly and simply as possible?

Casting offers a way to reproduce three-dimensional **technique**

forms, and the result can actually be a technical and aesthetic improvement

over the hand-fabricated prototype. I always cast the form

hollow and then solder on a back plate—I want the piece to

be "whole," yet light in weight.

Sometimes I emboss the surface of the fabricated

prototype to create a relief texture; that surface is replicated

in the cast form. Or I may apply a wire-brushed finish to

the completed casting. My more recent designs rely on

EARRINGS
Jester series
Sterling silver
Cast with hand-sanded
satin finish

labor-intensive hand-sanded finishes to complement the form.

I have always liked the look of hand-forged links, so I use my

own cast hammered links as well as commercial chain.

Chains are important visual, functional, and

metaphorical elements in my jewelry.

Sinuous and textural, the chain connects separate

parts to create a whole, as it

allows those parts to move

interdependently. My personal

experience often finds formal

expression in my jewelry. As I now balance the joys and

 demands of motherhood with those of the studio,

my vocabulary of forms has evolved. Shapes have become

softer, more organic, more sensuous.

Connections between forms create a seamless

structural unity. Each element is crucial to the whole.

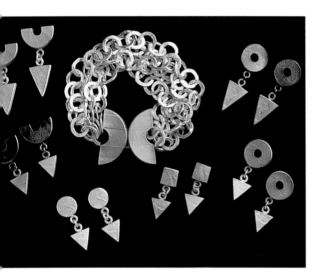

EARRINGS AND BRACELET
Sterling silver and gold plate
Cast, textured, and oxidized

EARRINGS, BRACELETS, AND PENDANT
Sterling silver, gold plate, and commercial chain
Cast and oxidized

BRACELET   *Jester series: Roller*
Sterling silver
Cast with hand-sanded satin finish

didi suydam

NECKLACE   *Free-Form series*
Sterling silver and gold plate

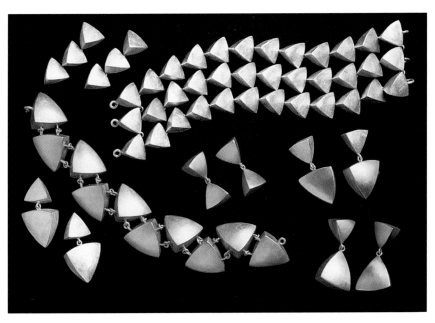

EARRINGS AND BRACELETS
Free-Form series: Earrings, Armadillo Bracelet, and Fat-Form Bracelet
Sterling silver and gold plate
Cast with hand-sanded satin finish

NECKLACE
Pod series
Sterling silver
and gold plate
Cast

EARRINGS AND BRACELETS   *Jester series*
Sterling silver and gold plate
Cast

EARRINGS   *Medieval Chandelier series*
Sterling silver, gold plate, and commercial chain
Cast and oxidized

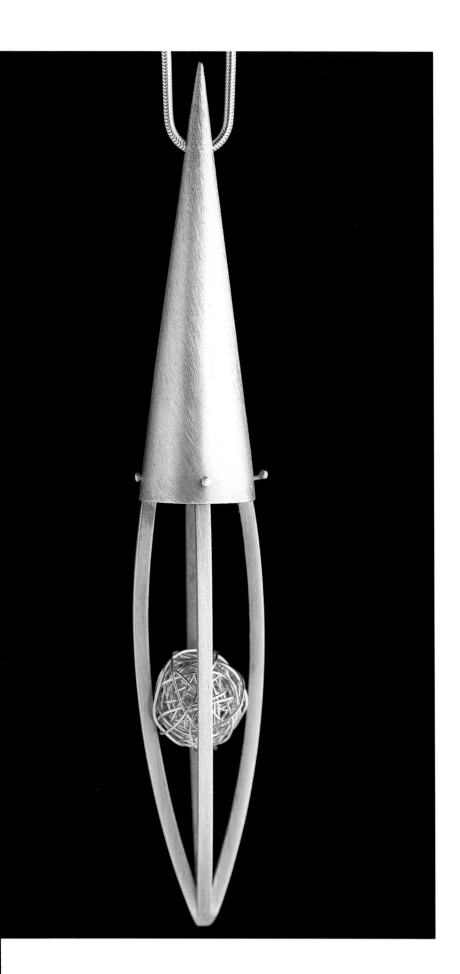

Architecture, industrial forms, and organic shapes influence Lorelei Hamm's jewelry design. In her early work she combined alternative materials such as rubber and silk-screened acrylic with traditional sterling silver and space-age niobium in designs for hard-edged, geometric jewelry. Using the refractive metal niobium, which is inherently light in weight, malleable, and easy to anodize, Hamm explored color and scale in her fibula pins and earrings.

Since 1981, Hamm has designed production and one-of-a-kind jewelry, as well as tables and tabletop objects. Her work has evolved in design, technique, and material. She now works almost exclusively in hollow forms made of sterling silver, exploring its tonal possibilities by texturing it, oxidizing it,

Lorelei Hamm

or contrasting it with gold or copper. Organic shapes juxtaposed with industrial structures are a recurring theme in her work. She favors formal circles and ovals, using sheet silver to create pointed, elongated ovoid forms or, most recently, the architectonics of her cone variations.

Hamm contrasts solid geometric shapes with linear patterns. She often places tangled balls of wire or elegant wire networks within a solid structure. Her recent bracelets, among her most satisfying work, continue this investigation of line. Industrial in design, each piece combines rhythm, proportion, movement, and stasis in an integrated structure.

Hamm defines jewelry as the intimate bond between the object of adornment and the wearer. Her jewelry projects an aura of mystery, suggesting powerful amulets, artifacts of an industrial age.

NECKLACE
Sterling silver and copper
Hollow constructed

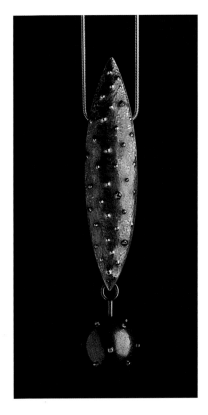

NECKLACE
Sterling silver
Hollow formed
and constructed

NECKLACE
14-karat gold and sterling silver
Fabricated and hollow formed

technique

In the past, my forms, joined using cold connection techniques, were primarily geometric and hard-edged. Inspired by themes of technology and industry, I incorporated many different materials—plastics, rubber, niobium—into each piece.

Today, I work with traditional metals and traditional techniques. I do not use stones or chemical patination, but rather the monotone hues that metal produces naturally. My imagery now is drawn from personal experience. I want to create a visual language for jewelry based on the organic, industrial, and cultural symbols that influence us all. For example, scars or suture marks, symbols of the pain and growth

PIN
18-karat gold and sterling silver
Fabricated

inherent in life, have become part of my

dialogue and indicate the direction of my work

to come.

I work with sterling silver, sometimes incorporating

18-karat gold or copper. I use hollow construction and

hollow forming techniques, fabrication, and casting to create

these pieces. Ninety-five per cent of my tools are hand

tools—I like the control of handworking each part of a piece

and prefer textures that can only be created by hand.

No two pieces ever look exactly the same.

RING BOX
14-karat gold and sterling silver
Constructed and fabricated

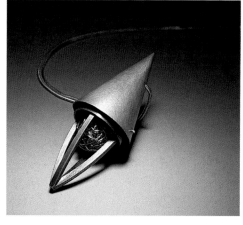

NECKLACE
14-karat gold and sterling silver
Hollow formed and fabricated

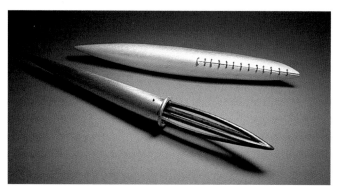

PINS
18-karat gold, fine silver, and sterling silver
Hollow formed and fabricated

NECKLACE
18-karat and 14-karat gold and sterling silver
Hollow formed and fabricated

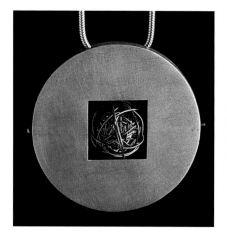

NECKLACE
18-karat gold and
sterling silver
Hollow constructed

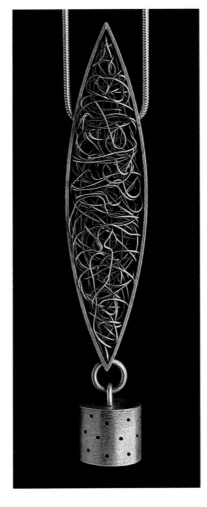

NECKLACE
Sterling silver
Fabricated and
hollow constructed

EARRINGS
Sterling silver
Cast and fabricated

lorelei hamm

BRACELETS
Sterling silver and bronze
Cast and fabricated

BRACELET
18-karat and 14-karat gold and sterling silver
Cast, hollow constructed, and fabricated

designing with alternative materials

Often when a jeweler chooses to work with unconventional materials—such as handmade paper, found objects, rubber, or graphite—he or she establishes a new idiom, inventing new structures for jewelry. Jocelyn Chateauvert, who designs jewelry based on her translucent abaca paper, and Thomas Mann, who creates a culture of techno-romantic jewelry, are just such jewelers.

Working with enamel, graphite, and mica, Joan Parcher's jewelry displays an economy of form inseparable from sensuous material. She tweaks our reverence for

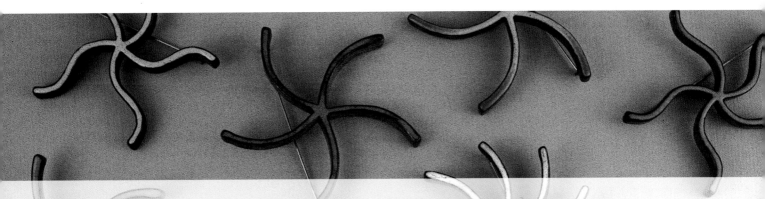

jewelry's conventions as she reinvents these forms in her spirited jewelry.

Boo Poulin has introduced a vocabulary of printed plastic, painted metal, and rubber parts to redefine what jewelry could and should be made from. Amy Anthony has also extended the parameters of jewelry design, using machine-tool technology and industrial materials to explore the intimacy of jewelry.

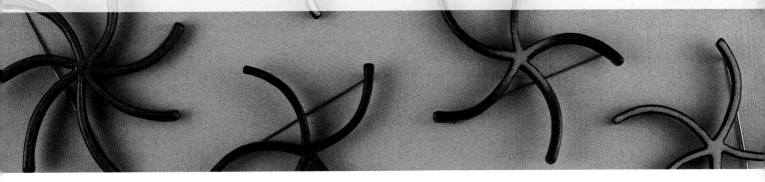

JOAN PARCHER
BROOCHES
Copper and enamel
Electroformed, enameled, and patinated

Laughter—effervescent, spontaneous, intelligent laughter—characterizes Jocelyn

Jocelyn Chateauvert

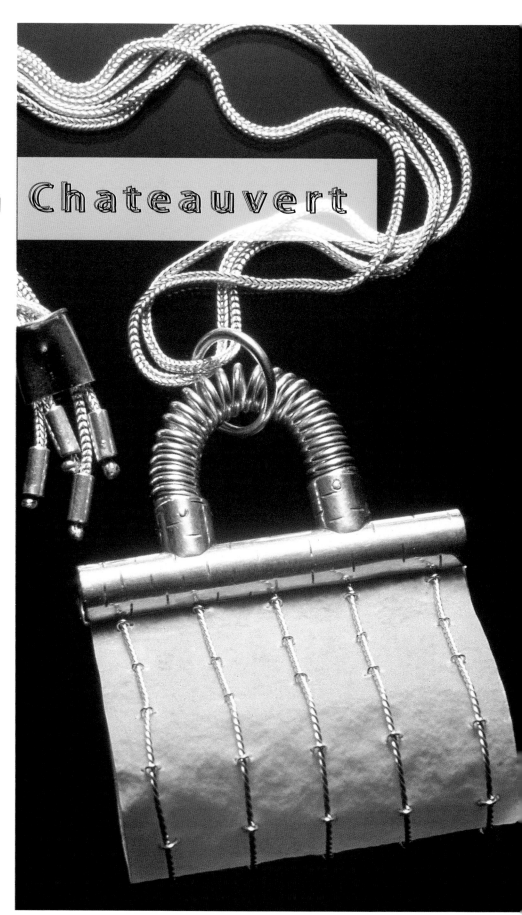

Chateauvert and her handmade paper jewelry collection. Most of her work is connected to a story with an element of humor. She celebrates paper's structure and translucency, complementing it with silver's opacity and solidity. The combination presents a yin-and-yang—the paper made from fiber and water, the metal forged from earth and fire. Her work challenges conventional definitions of jewelry.

Raised on the arts, Chateauvert was enrolled in classes at the Des Moines Art Center starting at age four. At the University of Iowa, she studied jewelry and metalsmithing, and also began her romance with handmade paper. She loved the physical paper-making process and the aesthetic qualities of paper, combining it with silver to create sculptural forms.

Her artist's residency at London's Middlesex Polytechnic affirmed her commitment to challenge the parameters of what jewelry could be. She spent four years refining the unlikely combination of paper and metal in jewelry.

Her work is sensuous on many levels. The tactile material invites touch. The structure of both the paper itself and its relationship to the metal is technically interesting and can also be richly evocative. For example, in "Eve, Clothes Optional," a layered fig leaf on a long supple chain, Chateauvert suggests an imagined narrative, the erotic sensation of paper against skin, and the private ritual of adornment.

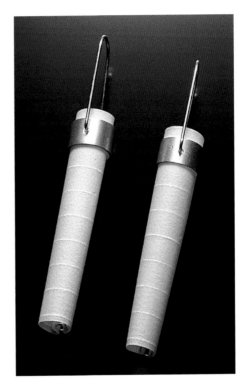

EARRINGS   *Cylinders*
Sterling and handmade paper
Fabricated

PENDANT   *Weekender*
Sterling silver, fine silver, and handmade paper
Fabricated

I usually start with drawings, but these are mere thumbnail sketches and only suggest a direction. From there my best success comes from directly working with paper and then looking for complementary metalwork. Of course, on occasion I get a total vision of a piece.

I work with abaca paper, a variation of a traditional paper made in the Philippines. It is archival, flexible, and naturally resistant to water. Although light in weight, it has solidity

technique

and presence. I make the paper in my studio, working with a Hollander beater, molds, a hydraulic press, and felts. I use an awl both to mark the silhouette for cutting and to define an edge by compressing the fibers. In other pieces, I prefer to leave a deckle edge. My concern in

EARRINGS *Niagara Falls*
Sterling silver and handmade paper
Fabricated

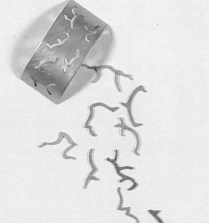

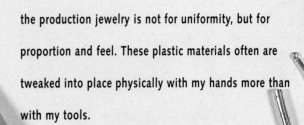

the production jewelry is not for uniformity, but for proportion and feel. These plastic materials often are tweaked into place physically with my hands more than with my tools.

After developing the paper elements and their relationship to the body, I then house them in the simplest possible metal lines. I fabricate the silver housing, often incorporating embossed or hammered surfaces. I enjoy hand-sawing and use the technique to graze slits in silver tubing or to make cutouts.

Paper is primary. It inspires me. Although I feel that I am still developing vocabulary for the work, my direction is clear. In moving from architectural to more complex organic constructed forms, with less metal housing, I invite more physical interaction between the object and the wearer. In the most interesting work, the paper has formal and structural autonomy.

jocelyn chateauvert

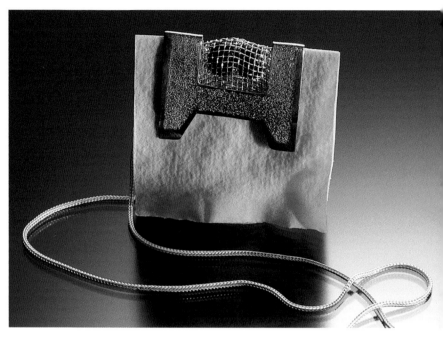

PENDANT *Rice and Beans*
Sterling silver, fine silver mesh, handmade paper, and beans
Embossed and fabricated

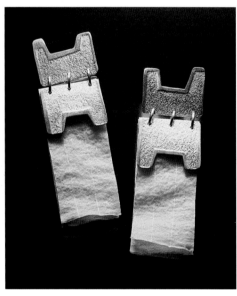

EARRINGS *RBE*
Sterling silver and handmade paper
Embossed and fabricated

PENDANT *Volume 1*
Sterling silver and handmade paper
Fabricated

EARRINGS *Leaf Forms*
Sterling silver and handmade paper
Fabricated

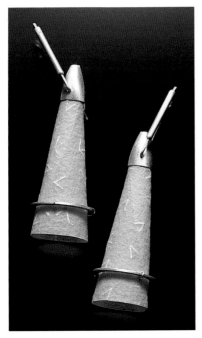

EARRINGS   *Twin Peaks*
Sterling silver and handmade paper
Fabricated

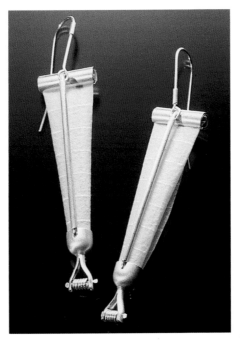

EARRINGS   *Speedy Vacs*
Sterling silver and handmade paper
Fabricated

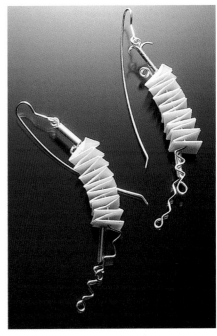

EARRINGS   *Jacks*
Sterling silver and handmade paper
Fabricated

PENDANT
Sterling silver and handmade paper
Fabricated

EARRINGS   *Handbags*
Sterling silver and handmade paper
Fabricated

PENDANT   *Eve, Clothes Optional*
Sterling silver and handmade paper
Fabricated

Boo Poulin

Boo Poulin's work is characterized by precise craftsmanship, spare forms, and richly articulated surfaces.

In the early 1980s, Poulin began her career by making a series of stainless steel pins with graphic tape incorporated on the surfaces. This unusual combination sparked an ongoing desire to redefine jewelry in terms of what it could and should be made of. She later developed custom colors and print patterns on plastic, and she created jewelry that incorporated printed plastic, painted metal, and rubber.

Although Poulin's finished pieces continue to be unconventional, her latest work marks a return to more traditional materials and techniques. Silver is cast, heavily textured, and oxidized; the silver forms are then combined with plastic or steel cable. These designs exhibit the same juxtaposition of extremes that has characterized her jewelry from the start. Poulin elevates the most basic of materials through the strength and simplicity of her design.

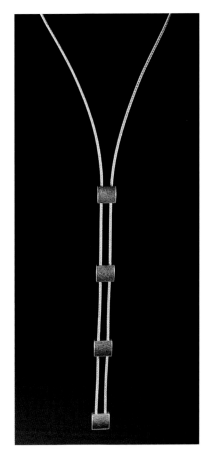

NECKLACE
Sterling silver and steel cable
Cast and fabricated

BRACELET
Sterling silver
Cast and fabricated

The design process for me is a progression of ideas that ultimately creates a unique visual language. Sometimes I will make very quick drawings that are often accompanied by words. Simultaneously, I collect materials that I find suggestive: rusted metal parts, hardware store paraphernalia, or even machine pieces, such as gears—in other words, whatever I might find that attracts me visually.

technique

In the past, I worked with small industrial shops that produced parts to my specifications; then I finished the jewelry in my studio. The finishing often included sanding, hand-coloring plastic, texturing metals, and some assembly. I used rubber O-rings as connectors, and I incorporated screws both for their visual interest and as a means of joining the alternative materials (plastic, aluminum, rubber) that I was fond of using at the time.

PIN
Sterling silver, plastic, and rubber
Die-cut and fabricated

Since I have returned to silver in my work, my

technical concerns have changed. Casting is now

my primary means of achieving an

inventory of shapes. I make prototypes

that are either fabricated in metal or carved in wax.

I work out all technical concerns at this stage:

mechanical   considerations are incorporated,

weight is   factored in, and proportions

are determined. Even though my primary material is

currently silver, my obsession with color and surface

remains. In order to finish my pieces, I file them heavily

to create an interesting surface, and I oxidize them to

change the color of the silver to a rich gray. Although

nothing is highly polished, everything shines.

BRACELET
Sterling silver
Cast and fabricated

NECKLACE
Sterling silver
Cast and fabricated

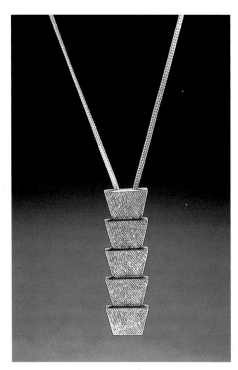

NECKLACE
Sterling silver
Cast and fabricated

BRACELETS
Sterling silver and steel
Cast and fabricated

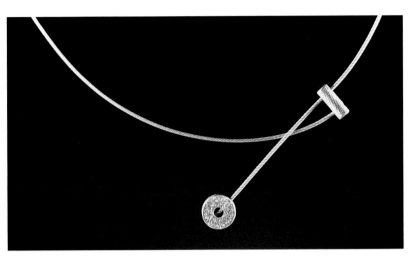

NECKLACE
Sterling silver and steel cable

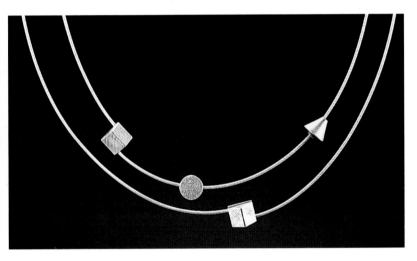

TWO NECKLACES
Sterling silver and steel cable
Cast and fabricated

EARRINGS
Sterling silver
Cast and
fabricated

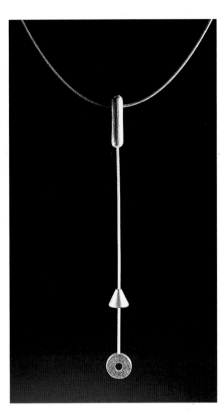

NECKLACE
Sterling silver and steel cable
Cast and fabricated

boo poulin

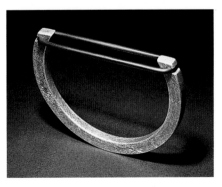

BRACELET
Sterling silver and rubber
Cast and fabricated

Thomas Mann

During the late 1970s and early 198⬦ Thomas Mann experimented with collage and assemblage, applying th⬦ quintessentially twentieth-century te⬦ niques to the creation of jewelry. Ou⬦ of these investigations he formulate⬦ vocabulary of material, technique, a⬦ design that he calls "techno-romant⬦ defined by romantic imagery made o⬦ nostalgic and high-tech materials, fr⬦ tintype photographs to printed circu⬦ boards. His collage technique allows⬦ Mann to layer several ideas and con⬦ cepts into a small physical space. Th⬦ found obje⬦ cornerstor⬦ and catalyst for each design, speaks ⬦ the serendipitous encounter.

During the formative years of the techno-romantic style, the "look" focused on found objects—salvage from the space and electronics industries, machine parts, and plastics. As the audience for the work grew, it became more difficult to find enough of this material. In the mid-1980s, Mann started to make parts that *appear* to be found objects.

Techno-romanticism is more than an aesthetic. It forms a language to express Mann's strongly held political and social views—he hopes to transform our relationship to technology, recognizing both our connection to and alienation from it. He wants his work to be evaluated on the basis of image and message content rather than the value of materials; thus he deliberately chooses to work with nonprecious metals—brass, bronze, stainless steel, copper, aluminum. (Sterling silver is the only exception.) Going beyond the usual expectations of adornment, his amulets express wearable ideas. His intent to provide as much aesthetic content as possible at an accessible price has contributed to the enormous success of his work.

PINS   *Caged Eye Photo*
Silver, brass, acrylic,
and photograph; Fabricated

PIN   *Hand*
Bronze, brass, and laminated Lucite
Fabricated

technique

I feel that I participate, in a metaphysical manner, in the delivery of meaning and definition to the tribe. I make little mechanisms for people to use to construct their own realities. I draw almost everything I make. Drawing is the stage at which the idea and the intention cross over from the possible to the probable. I start with design investigations for the one-of-a-kind pieces, and find within them the elements that will feed the production line. In the process of working at the bench,

I make design decisions about the prototype that will affect the look of the piece and the method of production. Often I discover a little fabrication trick.

The very nature of collage determines that cold connections form the primary fabrication technique. I use rivets, stitching, slots and tabs, and nuts and bolts to join the different

PIN *Collage Running House*
Brass, bronze, and laminated Lucite
Fabricated

elements and layers. Along with

traditional metalsmithing techniques, I use

die-forming, photo-etching, and sandblasting.

My attitude toward material, technique, and concept

defines the techno-romantic idiom. I work with a variety of

materials from different sources, in which each element contributes to an

integrated narrative and formal structure. A flat, chased graphic

background of brass, bronze, nickel, or silver is built up with

collage elements of various materials. With miniature bolts,

I attach laminated two-color acrylic slabs, cut as diagonal

striping. Perforated screening of various sizes and materials

serves as the matrix for attaching collage objects. These elements work together

to produce a dense surface of ornamentation with movement and color. Hearts

are a recurring image and theme in my work, as is containment. Small spaces

are often filled with entrapped or encapsulated objects.

The work is labor-intensive. It is simply not possible to make everything

by hand. Using tools and machinery to make the process cost-effective is simply

common sense. But it's important to me that the work maintains a high level of

technical quality and retains the spirit of the handmade process.

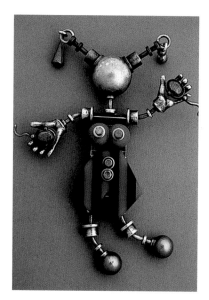

PIN *Fertility Goddess*
Silver, bronze, brass, laminated
Lucite, iron, and Micarta
Fabricated

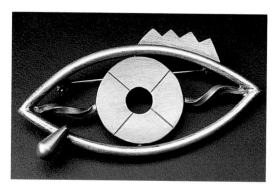

PIN *Eye*
Silver, brass, and nickel
Fabricated

thomas mann

BRACELETS *Locomotion*
Bronze
Constructed and fabricated

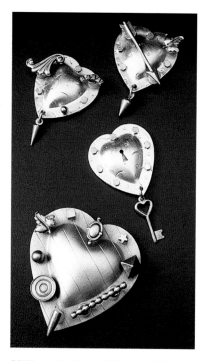

PINS *Collage Chamber Heart*
Silver, brass, bronze, and nickel
Die-formed and fabricated

EARRINGS *Collage Hand*
Nickel, brass, glass, and Lucite
Fabricated

MONEY CLIPS *Abstract*
Nickel and bronze
Fabricated

NECKLACE   *Three-D Heart*
Silver, brass, bronze, and copper
Die-formed and fabricated

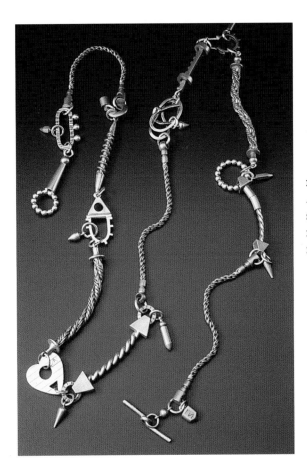

PIN
Collage Torso
Silver, bronze,
aluminum, and
stainless steel
Fabricated

PENDANT
ollage Chamber Heart
Silver, brass, bronze,
and nickel
Die-formed and
fabricated

NECKLACE
Abstract Charm
Silver, brass,
bronze, and nickel
Fabricated

Joan Parcher's earliest childhood memories are of designing and figuring out ways to make jewelry. At four years of age, she discovered wire-cutting pliers. Later, she collected discarded "junk" and, with a hammer and determination, formed it into rings and necklaces.

To this enduring passion for jewelry, Parcher joins a love for materials; her favorites include graphite, mica, other stones, and enamel. Her jewelry designs are based on an understanding of their physical nature. She loves the process of enameling and the color of opaque enamels. Her Graphite Pendulum pendant, carved on the lathe, demonstrates Parcher's fascination with cause and effect. The graphite pendulum leaves a smudged shadow that records its movement across the wearer's body.

Joan Parcher

She contemplates designs and materials, sometimes for years, before incorporating them into her working vocabulary. The concept of two opposite things, a positive and a negative shape, on the end of a cable first occurred to her in the 1970s. It was another decade, however, before she finally made the Ball and Hoop Neckpiece. The incubation period for her recent mica jewelry was even longer.

Although she works equally well with both organic and geometric forms, the quintessential Parcher aesthetic is based upon simple, functional, well-designed, wearable objects. She fabricates the complex geometry of the Polyhedron and Hoop neckpiece from a simple four-sided pyramidal commercial finding. The simplicity and spontaneity of her Flower earrings transcend cliché: she domes a precut copper shape, dusts it with enamel powder, adds a tumbled hematite bead, and then joins it to her own silver and gold earring finding. She reinvents the basic chain by using links of transparent mica. Parcher has wonderful fun giving pleasure through the jewelry she makes.

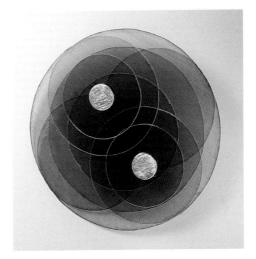

BROOCH   *Mica*
Sterling silver and mica
Pierced and fabricated

CHAIN   *Mica*
18-Karat gold and mica
Die-cut and fabricated

I like to learn about the nature of the materials that I work with. They inspire

me. I do lots of sketches and idea drawings, and I often have to

think about a piece for a long time before I actually make it. I use

simple shapes to allow the nature of the materials to predominate.

Graphite interests me because it makes a mark on almost everything

it touches. With mica, a lightweight, see-through stone, I can

make a thirteen-foot chain that is as light as a feather; or I can

layer it to make a transparent brooch.

The mica comes from India in sheets of varying thickness and colors,

from rose to slightly brown. I like to work with

the clearest available, which is silvery in tone.

technique

For the brooches, I lay out the design and score the surface with dividers—

or I use a template to mark the pattern of circles. Then I cut out the shape.

EARRINGS
Sterling silver and 24-karat vermeil
Cast and oxidized

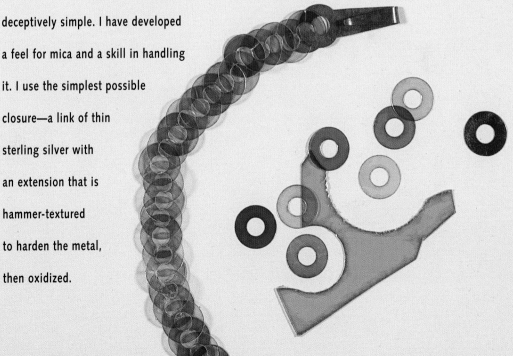

Scissors make the edge crack slightly; the jeweler's saw blade leaves a soft, flaky, silvery edge. Center discs of sterling silver join the overlapping circles to the backing.

I fabricate the chain from die-cut doughnut shapes of mica. The process is identical to the most basic loop-in-loop wire chain: two closed rings are joined with an open link, which is then glued with epoxy. Multiplying this basic unit, I can make a chain of any length. The technique is deceptively simple. I have developed a feel for mica and a skill in handling it. I use the simplest possible closure—a link of thin sterling silver with an extension that is hammer-textured to harden the metal, then oxidized.

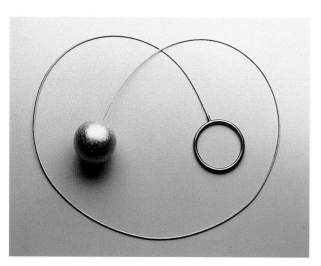

NECKPIECE   *Ball and Hoop*
24-karat gold leaf over sterling silver, and stainless steel
Fabricated and oxidized

BRACELETS
Copper and enamel
Electroformed, enameled, and patinated

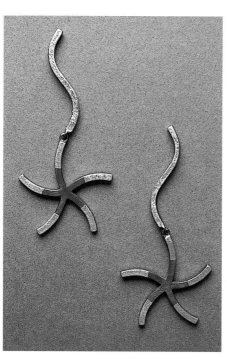

EARRINGS
Sterling silver and 24-karat vermeil
Cast and oxidized

PENDANT   [above and right]
Graphite Pendulum
Soft graphite, sterling silver, and stainless steel
Lathe-turned and fabricated

NECKLACES
Sterling silver
Cast

EARRINGS
Flower
Sterling silver, copper,
and enamel
Formed, enameled,
and oxidized

joan parcher

NECKPIECE   *Polyhedron and Hoop*
23-karat gold leaf over sterling silver,
and stainless steel
Cast, fabricated, and oxidized

BRACELET
Polka Dot
Sterling silver and copper
Enameled and oxidized

Machine-tool technology inspires Amy Anthony's precise, spare, yet playful brooches. Her machine aesthetic is fluently expressed in her materials—aluminum, steel, plastic—and in her design process, which she describes as series of decisions.

These decisions start with manipulation of the material. Anthony does not make drawings, but rather carves directly into the material with tool and die equipment, which includes horizontal and vertical mills, router, shaper,

Amy Anthony

and band saw. The machines introduce surface texture: grooves, scars, punches, scratches. Anthony then considers the direction of the piece. Often she will use traditional metalsmithing techniques to refine and complement the machined form. She may forge a surface to create a soft, broken, stressed edge, or she may file and sand the surface to remove the machine marks.

Imagery and content emerge from the process of making the piece: how one part is joined to another, how one part fits into another. Anthony describes her jewelry as drawings that exist in three dimensions; typically these "drawings" show a line in relation to a flat plane. She often presents a highly controlled, rigid relation between steel and aluminum, and then secures it with the most casual connection—a rubber band. Although the somber grays of stainless steel and aluminum reflect the subdued colors of the urban environment, Anthony introduces unexpected color by anodizing the aluminum.

When Anthony first set up her workshop, she cut out all her parts with a hacksaw and then filed them square. As she has acquired more tools and equipment, she has changed her method of production. Now she uses the band saw to cut out parts, mills them square, and then hand-finishes each part. Although the level of precision was better when she completed each step by hand, new

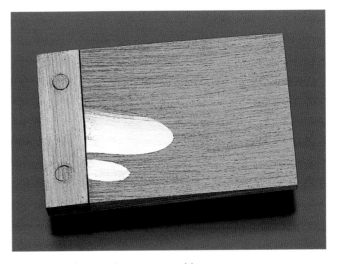

tools and techniques have increased her aesthetic choices. Her next leap in machine technology will be the computer. CNC (computerized numerical control) equipment will enable her to reproduce prototypes more easily and efficiently.

BROOCH
Aluminum and stainless steel
Hand- and machine-fabricated

ROOCH
Aluminum, brass, and Delrin
Hand- and machine-fabricated

I tend to make changes and choices that allow me to reproduce production work with ease. For example, I chose plastic as a base material for my latest pieces. It is stable, lightweight, and neutral in color. It is also easy to manipulate and much easier to cut than aluminum and stainless steel.

The design process starts with a block of Delrin stock. I use the band saw and a coarse blade to cut down its thickness. I really like the texture of the rip cut, which provides inspiration for developing the rest of the piece. I cut two parallel edges. Then I use the shaper to cut two skinny triangles with angled walls—this gives the illusion of two planes, one smooth and one textured.

technique

Working on the lathe, I drill a hole in the center of some round aluminum stock. Then I ream the hole, to obtain accurate size and a smooth finish. On the milling machine, I cut two flat parallel surfaces—so the stock is no longer circular in cross-section. By using the hacksaw and cutting

BROOCH
Aluminum, stainless steel, and string
Hand- and machine-fabricated

the stock at an angle, I change the circle to an oval.

I then remove all saw marks by machine- and

hand-sanding. I make a second, angled cut to

separate the oval washer from the stock.

Before joining the aluminum to the plastic,

I machine down the thickness of the plastic. To make the

cold connections, I drill the aluminum with a tap drill.

Using the aluminum as a template, I transfer the center

of the holes onto the plastic and drill them out with

a clearance drill. From the back of the brooch, I counter-

sink two flat-headed screws into the plastic and then

thread them into the aluminum. I solder the brooch

finding onto a screwhead, drill and tap a hole in the

plastic, and finally screw it in.

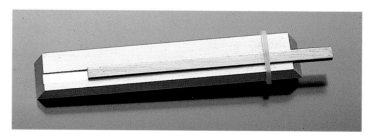

BROOCH
Aluminum, steel, and rubber band
Hand- and machine-fabricated

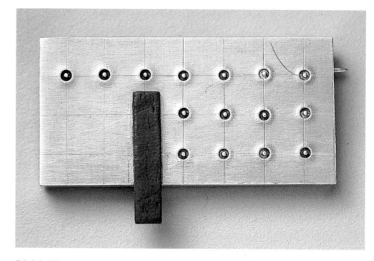

BROOCH
Aluminum and mahogany
Hand fabricated

amy anthony

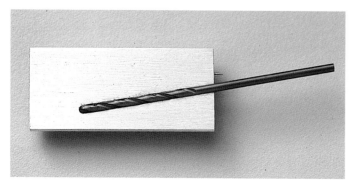

BROOCH
Aluminum and steel
Hand- and machine-fabricated

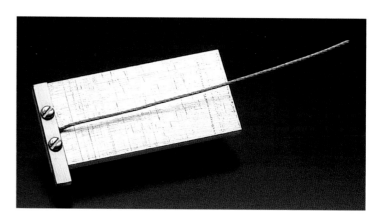

BROOCH
Aluminum, stainless steel, and steel
Hand- and machine-fabricated

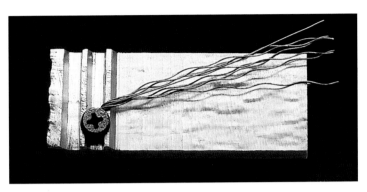

BROOCH
Aluminum and steel
Hand- and machine-fabricated

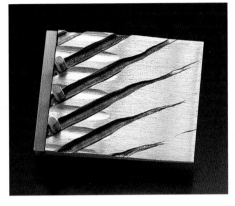

BROOCH
Aluminum, stainless steel, and ink
Hand- and machine-fabricated

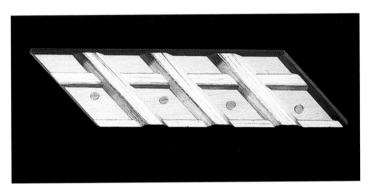

BROOCH
Aluminum and stainless steel
Hand- and machine-fabricated

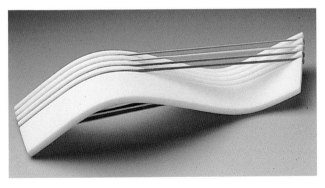

BRACELET
Teflon with colored rubber bands
Hand- and machine-fabricated

BROOCH
Stainless steel and Delrin
Hand- and machine-fabricated

Contributors

Jewelry Artists

Abrasha
pages 199, 218–223
P. O. Box 640283
San Francisco, CA 94109 USA

Amy Anthony
pages 270–275
1211 Titus Avenue
Rochester, NY 14617 USA

Chari Auerbach
pages 102–103, 106–107
CrystalMagic3645@aol.com
Chari lives in Port St. Lucie, Florida.
She is a talented seed bead artist,
but she also enjoys making other
types of beaded jewelry using stones,
minerals, pearls, and crystals. Along
with making her own jewelry, Chari
collects antique jewelry and is an
expert on antique crystal jewelry.

Terry L. Carter
page 112–113
Lmntre04@aol.com
Terry is from Muncie, Indiana. When
she isn't busy home schooling her
four children, she enjoys making
natural stone, mineral, and pearl
jewelry. Terry has incorporated
jewelry making in many areas of her
active life including teaching the
youth at her church to make jewelry
and also making jewelry for fund-
raising events.

Jocelyn Chateauvert
pages 246–251
123 1st Avenue South
Mount Vernon, IA 52314 USA

Rhona Farber
pages 104–105
www.overthemoonjewelry.com
rhona@overthemoonjewelry.com
Rhona operates her small jewelry
business, Over the Moon Jewelry,
from South Florida. However, her
hand-crafted bead and wire jewelry
can be found in boutiques and specialty shops throughout the United
States as well as around the world.
Rhona also sells her work through her
website.

Kate Ferrant Richbourg
page 55
kate@beadshop.com
Kate is a well-known jewelry instructor who teaches a variety of jewelry
techniques both nationally and at The
Beadshop in Palo Alto, California.
Kate teaches classes in beading, wire
jewelry, metalsmithing, and metal
clay. She is probably best known for
her wirework skills.

Michael Good Design
pages 212–217
P. O. Box 788
Rockport, ME 04856 USA

Lorelei Hamm
pages 225, 238–243
153 Garfield Place #4L
Brooklyn, NY 11215 USA

Barbara Heinrich
pages 200–205
P. O. Box 503
Pittsford, NY 14534 USA

Suzanne and Gary Helwig
pages 100–101, 108–109, 114–115
www.wigjig.com
custsrv@wigjig.com
*Suzanne and Gary are from Arlington,
Virginia. Both are actively involved
in their family-run business, Wig Jig,
where they sell their own wire jigs as
well as beading and wire supplies
through their website and at trade
shows. Their business developed from
a love of making jewelry, which they
continue to do by combining wire and
beads in their unique jewelry designs.*

Daphne D. Hess
pages 87, 110–111
www.members.tripod.com/ddhess
flmn579@cs.com
*Daphne D. Hess, known simply as
D.D. by many of her friends, is a
glass artist from Hobe Sound, Florida.
Though she specializes in lampwork
beads which she creates using an
oxygen and propane torch, D.D. also*
*makes beautiful fused glass jewelry
and home accessories. She sells her
work both retail and wholesale
through bead shops, galleries, art
shows, and her website.*

Reiko Ishiyama
pages 226–231
252 West 30th Street #9B
New York, NY 10001 USA

Michelle Lambert
page 116–117
www.jewelrymaking.about.com
mlambert@roadrunner.nf.net
*Michelle is from St. John's,
Newfoundland, in Canada. Besides
working with stone and pearl beads,
Michelle also makes many of her
own beads with polymer clay. She
is very active in the online jewelry
making community and cohosts
weekly chats at About.com's jewelry
making site.*

Thomas Mann
pages 258–263
1810 Magazine Street
New Orleans, LA 70130 USA

Joan A. Parcher
pages 245, 264–269
165 Arlington Avenue
Providence, RI 02906 USA

Janice Parsons

page 37

www.beadshop.com

ceo@beadshop.com

Janice is CEO and owner of The Beadshop, located in Palo Alto, California. After running a successful bead shop for many years, Janice expanded her business and opened www.beadshop.com where she sells beading supplies as well as kits through the Internet. She also makes beautiful beaded jewelry and specializes in pearls and pearl knotting.

Boo Poulin

pages 252–257

36 Saint Paul #5W

Rochester, NY 14604 USA

Didi Suydam

pages 232–237

58 Willow Street

Providence, RI 02909 USA

Kathryn L. Timmerman

pages 206–211

P.O. Box 3072

La Jolla, CA 92038 USA

Photographers

Abrasha

pages 219–220, 222–223

James Beards

pages 264–266, 268–269

Roger Birn

pages 232–234 236–237

Robert Blake

pages 238, 242–243

Bobbie Bush

www.bobbiebush.com

pages 8–119

Tim Callahan

pages 200–202, 204–205

Will Crocker

pages 258–260, 262–263

Dennis Dal Covey

pages 210–211

James Dee

pages 226–228, 230–231

Ralph Gabriner

pages 205, 262

Walter Jebe
page 219

Nick Juran
page 206

Koichiro Kamoji
pages 239–240, 242–243

Peter Krumhart
pages 246–248, 250–251

Carol Miller
page 217

Woody Packard
pages 270–272, 274–275

Gerald Perrone
page 262

George Plattetter
page 254

George Post
page 254

Joseph Schuyler
page 243

Helen Shirk
pages 208, 211

Jeff Slack
pages 213, 216

Jamie Stillings
page 257

Kathe Timmerman
pages 207, 210–211

TKO Studio
page 210

TPS Visual Communications
page 212

Ronnie Tsai
pages 218, 223

Ron Wu
pages 252–254, 256–257

Resources

550 Silver & Supply
(505) 598-5322
www.metalworks.com
Metal findings, wire, and beads

Artgems Inc.com
3850 East Baseline Road, Suite 119
Mesa, AZ 85206 USA
(480) 545-6009
www.artgemsinc.com
artgems@artgemsinc.com
*Artgems Inc. has a store in Mesa,
Arizona, but they also offer a huge
collection of beads, charms, and findings from around the world through
their website. In addition to supplies,
they sell tools and videos as well.
Stop by their website to see their
"Deal of the Day."*

Auntie's Beads
(888) 844-7657
www.auntiesbeads.com
*Beads and general jewelry making
supplies*

The Bead Company of Australia
+61 2 9546 4544 (extension 25)
www.beadcompany.com.au
*Beads and general jewelry making
supplies*

The Bead Shop
21a Tower Street
London WC2H 9NS
UK
+44 0207 240 0931

The Bead Warehouse
(301) 565-0487
www.thebeadwarehouse.com
*Stone beads and general jewelry mak-
ing supplies*

Beads Unlimited
+44 01273 740777
www.beadsunlimited.co.uk
*UK supplier of beads and general
jewelry making supplies*

Beadalon
(800) 824-9473
www.beadalon.com
*Beadalon beading wire and general
jewelry-making supplies*

Beadbox
(480) 976-4080
www.beadlovers.com
*Beads and general jewelry making
supplies*

BeadFX
(877) 473-2323
www.beadfx.com
*Canadian supplier of glass, crystal,
and seed beads*

Beadgems
202 Swanshurst Lane
Moseley, Birmingham
West Midlands, B13 0AW
UK
+44 0121 778 6314
www.beadgems.com

Beadshop.com
158 University Avenue
Palo Alto, CA 94301 USA
(650) 328-7925
www.beadshop.com
webmanager@beadshop.com
Beadshop.com is the website of The Bead Shop, which also has a storefront in Palo Alto, California. Not only do they offer a huge selection of quality beads, findings, and tools, but they also make their own jewelry kits and provide classes in a wide variety of jewelry techniques from metalsmithing to beading.

CGM
(800) 426-5246
www.cgmfindings.com
Wire, metal beads, and findings

Daphne D. Hess
Handcrafted Beads
Hobe Sound, FL USA
(772) 546-8960
www.members.tripod.com/ddhess
Flmn579@cs.com
This glass artist specializes in flameworked glass, beads, and jewelry. You can either purchase her lampwork beads wholesale or retail through her website or give her a call.

Fire Mountain Gems
(800) 355-2187
www.firemoutaingems.com
General jewelry making supplies

HHH Enterprises
(800) 777-0218
www.hhhenterprises.com
General jewelry making supplies

HobbyCraft
Stores throughout the UK
Head Office
Bournemouth
UK
+44 1202 596 100

The House of Orange
(250) 544-0127
www.houseoforange.biz
Canadian supplier of beads and general jewelry making supplies

John Lewis
Stores throughout the UK
Flagship Store
Oxford Street
London W1A 1EX
UK
+44 20 7269 7711
www.johnlewis.co.uk

Katie's Treasures
+61 2 4956 3435
www.katiestreasures.com.au
Australian supplier of beads and general jewelry making supplies

Kernowcrafts Rocks & Gems Limited
Bolingey
Perranporth
Cornwall TR6 0DH
UK
+44 01872 573 888
www.kernocraft.com

Manchester Minerals
Georges Road
Stockport
Cheshire SK4 1DP
UK
+44 0161 477 0435
www.gemcraft.co.uk

Rio Grande
7500 Bluewater Road NW
Albuquerque, NM 87121-1962 USA
(800) 545-7566
www.riogrande.com
info@riogrande.com
Whether you need beading supplies or professional casting equipment, Rio Grande has a tremendous selection of products for the jewelry maker. Either shop online or contact them for one of their catalogs: Gems & Findings, Tools & Equipment, or Display & Packaging.

Shipwreck Beads
(360) 754-2323
www.shipwreck-beads.com
General jewelry making supplies

Soft Flex Company
(707) 938-3539
www.softflextm.com
Soft Flex beading wire and general jewelry making supplies

South Pacific Wholesale Co.
(800) 338-2162
www.beading.com
Stone beads and general jewelry making supplies

Space Trader
+61 03 9534 5012
www.spacetrader.com.au
Australian supplier of beads and general jewelry making supplies

Wig Jig
P. O. Box 5306
Arlington, VA 22205 USA
(800) 579-WIRE
www.wigjig.com
custsrv@wigjig.com
Wig Jig is probably best known for its numerous wire jigs that allow you to create your own wire jewelry components and findings. However, they sell a variety of supplies, including beads, wire, tools, findings, books, and videos for jewelry makers. Their website offers a way to shop on line as well as many pages of free jewelry tutorials.

Wire-Sculpture.com
(601) 636-0600
www.wiresculpture.com
Wire and general jewelry supplies

United States

Albright Knox Art Gallery
1285 Elmwood Avenue
Buffalo, NY 14222 USA
(716) 882-8700

American Artisan
4231 Harding Road
Nashville, TN 37205 USA
(615) 298-4691

American Pie
327 South Street
Philedelphia, PA 19147 USA
(215) 351-8100

Atypic
333 West Brown Deer Road
Milwaukee, WI 53217 USA
(414) 351-0333

Connell Gallery
333 Buckhead Avenue
Atlanta, GA 30305 USA
(414) 261-1712

De Novo
250 University Avenue
Palo Alto, CA 94301 USA
(415) 327-1256

Fireworks
210 First Avenue South
Seattle, WA 98104 USA
(206) 682-8707

Freehand
8413 West Third Street
Los Angles, CA 90048 USA
(213) 655-2607

Gallery I/O
1812 Magazine Street
New Orleans, LA 70130 USA
(504) 581-2111

Jewelers' Werk Galerie
2000 Pennsylvania Avenue, NW
Washington, DC 20006 USA
(202) 293-0249

Joanne Rappo Gallery
The Hand and the Spirit
4222 North Marshall Way
Scottsdale, AZ 85251 USA
(602) 949-1262

**Linda Richman Jewelry at
Katie Gingrass Gallery**
241 North Broadway
Milwaukee, WI 53202 USA
(414) 289-0855

Mindscape
1506 Sherman Avenue
Evanston, IL 60201 USA
(847) 864-2660

Mobilia
358 Huron Avenue
Cambridge, MA 02138 USA
(617) 876-2109

Motto
17 Brattle Street
Cambridge, MA 02138 USA
(617) 868-8448

Museum of Modern Art
MOMA Store
44 West 53rd Street
New York, NY 10019 USA
(212) 708-9700

Nancy Margolis Gallery
367 Fore Street
Portland, ME 04101 USA
(207) 775-3822

Nancy Sachs Gallery
7700 Forsyth
St. Louis, MO 63105 USA
(314) 727-7770

Nina Liu and Friends
24 State Street
Charleston, SC 29401 USA
(803) 722-2744

Objects of Desire Gallery
3704 Lexington Road
Louisville, KY 40207 USA
(502) 896-2398

Philip David
968 Farmington Avenue
West Hartford, CT 06107 USA
(203) 232-6979

Pistachio's
One East Delaware
Chicago, IL 60611 USA
(312) 988-9433

Ragazzi's Flying Shuttle
607 First Avenue
Seattle, WA 98104 USA
(206) 343-3101

San Francisco Museum of Modern Art
151 Third Street
San Francisco, CA 94103 USA
(415) 357-4000

Shaw Gallery
100 Main Street
Northeast Harbor, ME 14662 USA
(207) 276-5000

Susan Cummins Gallery
12 Miller Avenue
Mill Valley, CA 94941 USA
(415) 383-1512

Takashimaya
693 Fifth Avenue
New York, NY 10022 USA
(800) 753-2038

Twist
30 NW 23rd Place #101
Portland, OR 97210 USA
(503) 224-0334

The Works
303 Cherry Street
Philadelphia, PA 19106 USA
(215) 922-7775

International

Artwalk
Piazza Motta 1
6612 Ascona
Switzerland

Barneys Japan Co. Ltd.
3-14-1 Shijuku-ku
Tokyo 160
Japan

Designers Guild
277 Kings Road
London SW35EN
UK

Electrum Gallery
21 South Moulton Street W1
London
UK

Electrum Gallery
21 South Moulton Street W1
London
UK

Galerie V+V
Bauernmarkt 19
1010 Vienna
Austria

Rox/Pithelwaite and Row-Thorpe
61 1A Barnscleuth Square
Elizabeth Bay (Sydney), NSW
Australia

Sandra Ainsley Gallery
Exchange Tower 2
1st Canadian Place, Box 262
Toronto, ON
Canada M5X1B5

Shelley Tadman Gallery
408 Academy Road
Winnipeg, Manitoba
Canada R3N0B9

Spektrum
Turkenstr. 37, Ruckgebaude
80799 Munich
Germany

Retail Craft Shows

February
The Coconut Grove Arts Festival
South Bay Shore Drive and
McFarlane Road
Coconut Grove, FL 33233 USA

American Craft Council (ACC)
Craft Fair
Baltimore Convention Center and
Hyatt Regency Inner Harbor
Baltimore, MD USA

March
ACC Craft Fair
Georgia Dome
Atlanta, GA USA

April
Smithsonian Craft Show
National Building Museum
401 F Street, NW
Washington, DC USA

ACC Craft Fair
Arena, St. Paul Civic Center
St. Paul, MN USA

June
ACC Craft Fair
Eastern States Exposition
West Springfield, MA USA

ACC Craft Fair
Greater Columbus Convention Center
Columbus, OH USA

July
Ann Arbor Street Art Fair
The Original Juried Fair
Ann Arbor, MI USA

August
The Evanston and Glenbrook Hospitals
American Craft Exposition
Henry Crown Sports Pavilion
Evanston, IL USA

ACC Craft Fair
Fort Mason Center
San Francisco, CA USA

November
Philadelphia Museum of Art
Craft Show
Pennsylvania Convention Center
Philadelphia, PA USA

December
ACC Craft Fair
Tampa Convention Center
Tampa, FL USA

ACC Craft Fair
Charlotte Convention Center
Charlotte, NC USA

About the Authors

Deborah Krupenia is an artist, metalsmith, instructor, and writer. Her work is represented in galleries nationwide and has been published in *American Craft*, *Metalsmith*, and *Ornament* magazines. She has taught jewelry courses at the De Cordova Museum School in Lincoln, Massachusetts, the School of the Museum of Fine Arts in Boston, and the Massachusetts College of Art. She lives in Cambridge, Massachusetts, with the feline goldsmith Cellini.

Tammy Powley is a writer, artist, and teacher. She has written craft articles for magazines; how-to projects for her jewelry-making website at About.com; and literary pieces for her own pleasure. Tammy has always been creative and often made her own jewelry while a teenager. She found her way to designing jewelry in 1989 when she attended a rock show and then decided to make jewelry for Christmas presents. Soon friends and co-workers asked if her work was for sale, and she ended up selling and remaking all of her Christmas gifts. A few months later, she started a jewelry business. She still continues to sell her finished jewelry in specialty shops and galleries. Besides working with beads, Tammy also enjoys fused glass and wirework. She currently resides in Port St. Lucie, Florida, with her husband, Michael, and a house full of dogs and cats.

Jessica Wrobel began her professional life as a costumer and paper and fiber artist, retailing her handcrafts in boutiques throughout New England and teaching art to the students of the ARC of Haverhill, Massachusetts, and Second Step/YMCA of Lawrence, Massachusetts. She was further able to explore the rich world of decorative techniques when she authored *The Paper Jewelry Book*, *The Crafter's Recipe Book*, and *Quick and Easy Flower Design* (Quarry Books 2005).

About the Author

Jessica Wrobel is one of the most exciting and innovative designers working today. Wrobel's highly successful studio work is well known for a wide variety of fine art, and features hand-marbled papers and fabrics, custom-designed clothing, jewelry, home accessories, and fresh florals. Wrobel devotes much of her time to teaching community art classes, in expression of her strong belief that art should be shared.

Acknowledgments

With special thanks to Tara, for her lovely hands; Mary McCarthy, whose inspiration led me down this path; and Mom and Dad, for letting me be who I am.

Dedicated to Tom, with love.

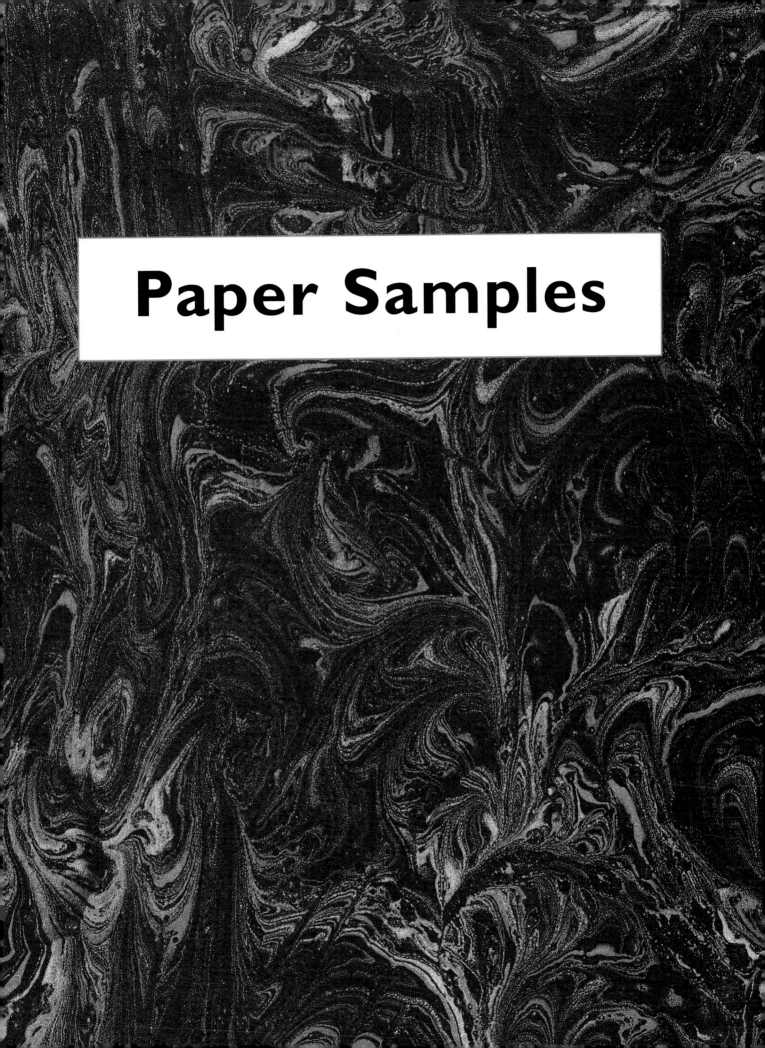

Paper Samples

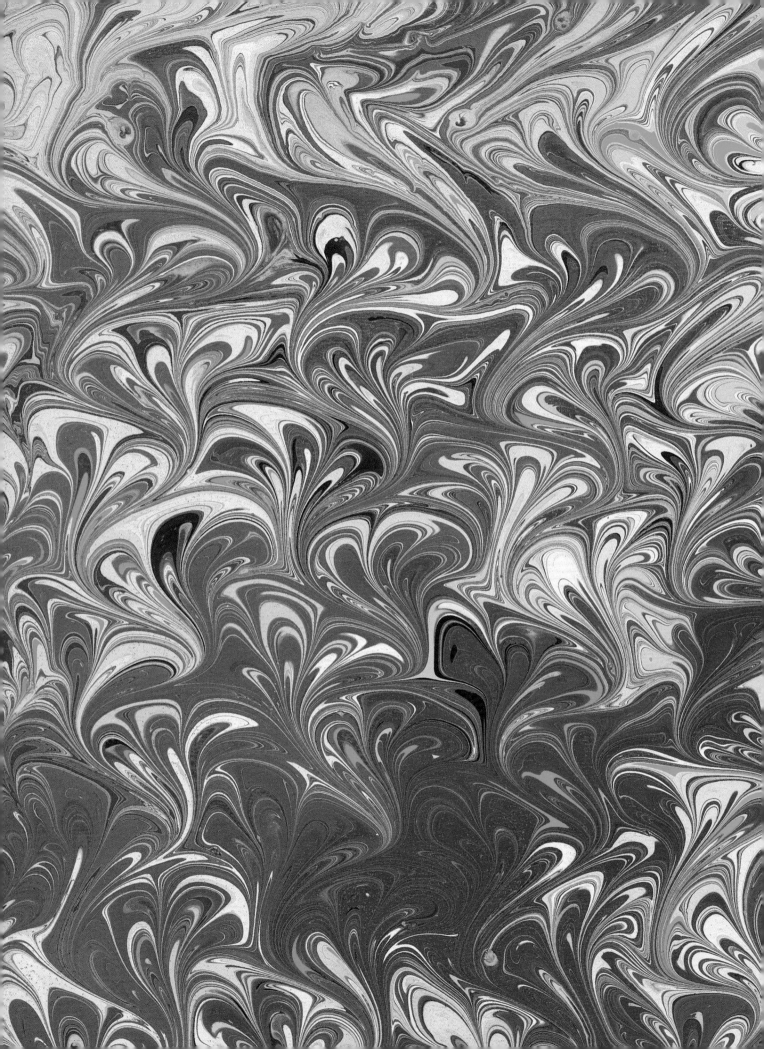

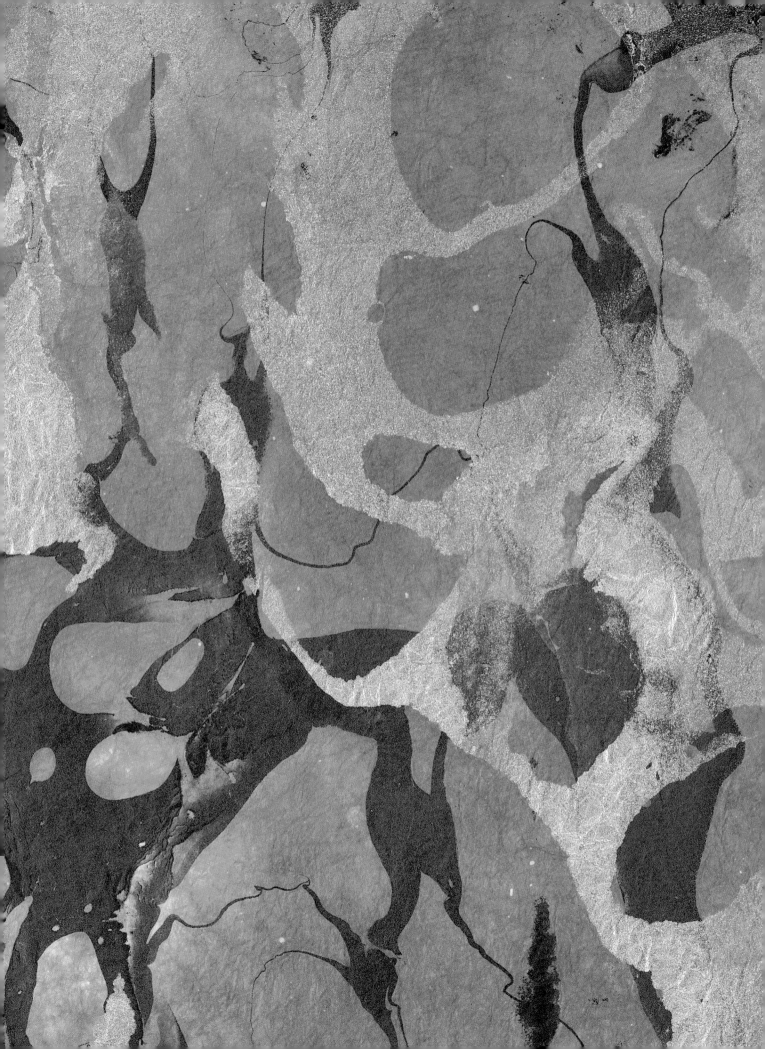

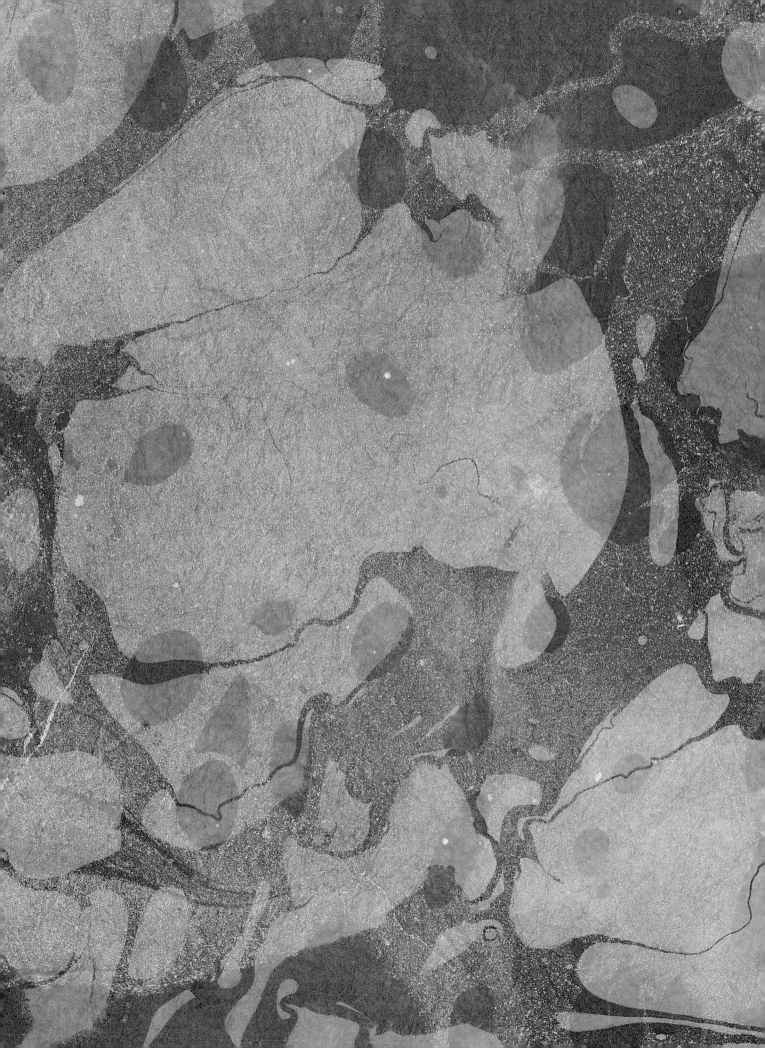

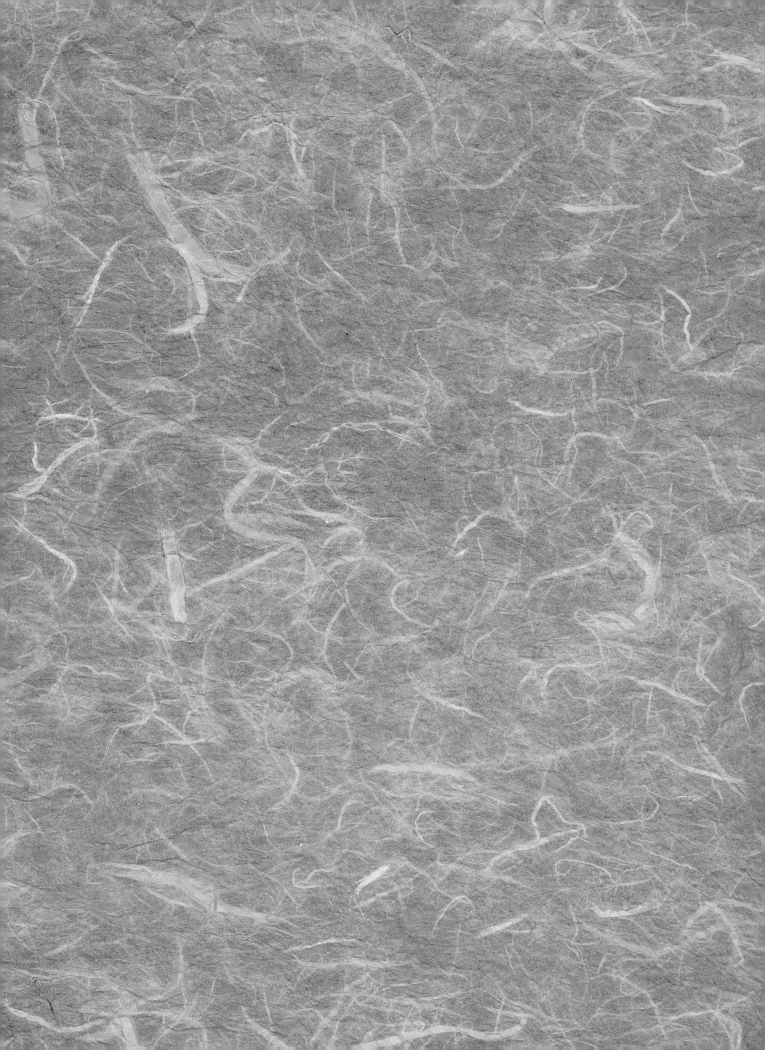